Nurturing Character in the Classroom

Ethical Judgment

EthEx Series Book 2

Nurturing Character in the Classroom, EthEx Series

    Ethical Sensitivity
    Ethical Judgment
    Ethical Motivation
    Ethical Action

CURRICULUM & COURSE-BASED TEXTS & RESOURCES DIVISION

Alliance for Catholic Education Press
at the University of Notre Dame

Nurturing Character in the Classroom

Ethical Judgment

EthEx Series Book 2

Darcia Narvaez, Ph.D.
Tonia Bock, Ph.D.

ALLIANCE FOR CATHOLIC EDUCATION PRESS
AT THE UNIVERSITY OF NOTRE DAME

Notre Dame, Indiana

Copyright © 2009

Alliance for Catholic Education Press
at the University of Notre Dame
158 IEI Building
Notre Dame, IN 46556
http://www.nd.edu/~acepress

Text design by Tonia Bock
Cover design by Mary Jo Adams Kocovski

ISBN: 978-0-9819501-1-2

Library of Congress Cataloging-in-Publication Data

Narvaez, Darcia.
  Ethical judgment / Darcia Narvaez, Tonia Bock.
     p. cm. -- (Nurturing character in the classroom, EthEx series ; bk. 2)
  Includes bibliographical references.
  Summary: "Provides a framework and instructional materials for integrating ethical education, specifically ethical
judgment, into the middle school classroom and curriculum"--Provided by publisher.
  ISBN 978-0-9819501-1-2 (pbk. : alk. paper)
 1. Moral education (Middle school)--United States. 2. Ethics--Study and teaching (Middle school)--United States. I.
Bock, Tonia. II. Title.

  LC268.N238 2009
  370.11'4--dc22
                                     2009004061

This book was printed on acid-free paper.

Printed in the United States of America.

Table of Contents

Foreword   *vii*

Preface   *ix*

Acknowledgments   *xi*

Introduction to the Ethical Expertise Model (EthEx)   1
    Purpose and Goals of the EthEx Model   3
    Should Teachers Teach Values?   4
    What Should Be Taught?   9
    How Should Character Be Taught?   20
    Who Decides Which Values to Teach?   24
    What Is the Student's Role?   25
    When Should Character Be Taught?   27
    How Ethical Process Skills Fit With Virtues   29
    References   33

Nurturing Ethical Judgment   35
    Organization of Materials   36
    Ethical Judgment Overview   39
    EJ-1: Reasoning Generally   46
    EJ-2: Reasoning Ethically   63
    EJ-3: Understanding Ethical Problems   77
    EJ-4: Using Codes and Identifying Judgment Criteria   94
    EJ-5: Understanding Consequences   105
    EJ-6: Reflecting on the Process and Outcome   119
    EJ-7: Coping   131
    Ethical Judgment Appendix   151

About the Authors   179

Foreword

For the past several years my colleagues and I at the University of Minnesota, in partnership with the Minnesota Department of Children, Families and Learning, have been developing a model for character education in the middle grades that we call "Community Voices and Character Education." Here are the six key characteristics of our model.

First, we adopt a <u>skills-based understanding</u> of moral character. This is not a new idea. Plato believed that the just person is like an artisan who has particular, highly-cultivated skills that have been developed through training and practice (Plato, 1987). Persons of good character, then, have better developed skills in four areas: ethical sensitivity, ethical judgment, ethical motivation, and ethical action (Narvaez, Mitchell, Endicott, & Bock, 1999). For example, experts in the skills of Ethical Sensitivity are better at quickly and accurately "reading" a moral situation and determining what role they might play (Narvaez & Endicott, 2009). Experts in the skills of Ethical Judgment have many tools for solving complex moral problems (Narvaez & Bock, 2009). Experts in the skills of Ethical Motivation cultivate an ethical identity that leads them to prioritize ethical goals (Narvaez & Lies, 2009). Experts in the skills of Ethical Action know how to keep their "eye on the prize," enabling them to stay on task and take the necessary steps to get the ethical job done (Narvaez, 2009). Our approach to character development, then, insists on a holistic understanding of the moral person (Narvaez, Bock, & Endicott, 2003). It views character as a set of component skills that can be cultivated to high levels of expertise.

Expertise is a notion that has gained prominence among educational researchers (e.g., Sternberg, 1998, 1999). According to this view, children move along a continuum from novice-to-expert in each content domain that they study. Unlike novices, experts have larger, more complex and better organized knowledge (Chi, Glaser, & Farr, 1988; Sternberg, 1998). Experts see the world differently (Neisser, 1967). Their extensive pattern matching capabilities allow experts to notice things that novices miss (Novick, 1988). Experts possess well-developed sets of procedural skills. Unlike novices, experts know *what* knowledge to access, *which* procedures to apply, *how* to apply them, and *when* it is appropriate (Abernathy & Hamm, 1995; Hogarth, 2001).

Second, to help children develop character skills in the way that experts do, we adopt a <u>scientifically-based</u>, cognitive approach to <u>learning and teaching</u> that assumes that children actively construct representations of the world (Narvaez, 2002; Piaget, 1932/1965, 1952, 1970). <u>Best practice instruction</u> provides opportunities for students to develop more accurate and better organized representations and the procedural skills required to use them (Anderson, 1989). Like the expert, students learn to master the defining features and underlying structures of a domain through practice that is focused, extensive, and coached (Ericsson & Charness, 1994; Ericsson, Krampe, & Tesch-Roemer, 1993). The educator provides authentic learning experiences that are structured according to what we know about levels of apprenticeship (Marshall, 1995; Rogoff, Baker-Sennett, Lacasa, & Goldsmith, 1995).

Third, our model insists that character development be <u>embedded within standards-driven academic instruction</u>, for ultimately this is the only way character education will be sustained.

Fourth, character should be <u>taught across the curriculum in every subject and activity</u>, for character skills are required not in isolation but throughout every encounter in life.

Fifth, our model opens character education to <u>greater accountability</u>, in the sense that skills are teachable and progress toward mastery can be measured.

Sixth, a curricular approach to character education must be an <u>intentional collaboration</u> with "community voices." After all, students are apprentices <u>to the community</u>. The issue of "whose values will be taught?" is best approached by embedding educational goals within the value commitments of particular communities.

Does this model work? Our preliminary data are quite promising. For example, classrooms using our approach showed increases in scores on prosocial responsibility, ethical identity, and prosocial risk-taking, while a comparison group did not.

In summary, moral character is best thought of as a set of teachable, ethically-relevant skills. Ethical skill instruction should be embedded in standards-driven pedagogy. Ethical skills should be taught across the curriculum and cultivated by community voices. With such an education, students will develop schemas of goodness and of justice. They will learn routines of helping and of reasoning. They will learn skills of leadership and of commitment. With these skills they can take responsibility for ethical action in their neighborhoods and in their communities. They will be energized by memories of personal ethical action. With these skills, students are empowered to be active citizens who will make the fate of the nation their own.

Speech at the Whitehouse Conference on Character and Community
Darcia Narvaez, Ph.D.
Associate Professor, University of Notre Dame
June 2002

References

Abernathy, C. M., & Hamm, R. M. (1995). *Surgical intuition*. Philadelphia: Hanley & Belfus.

Anderson, L. M. (1989). Learners and learning. In M. C. Reynolds (Ed.), *Knowledge base for the beginning teacher* (pp. 85-99). Oxford: Pergamon Press.

Chi, M. T. H., Glaser, R., & Farr, M. (1988*). The nature of expertise*. Hillsdale, NJ: Erlbaum.

Ericsson, K. A., & Charness, N. (1994). Expert performance: Its structure and acquisition. *American Psychologist, 49*, 725-747.

Ericsson, K. A., Krampe, R. T., & Tesch-Roemer, C. (1993). The role of deliberate practice in the acquisition of expert performance. *Psychological Review, 100*(3), 363-406.

Hogarth, R. M. (2001). *Educating intuition*. Chicago: University of Chicago Press.

Marshall, S. P. (1995). *Schemas in problem solving*. Cambridge: Cambridge University Press.

Narvaez, D. (2002). Does reading moral stories build character? *Educational Psychology Review, 14*(2), 155-171.

Narvaez, D. (2009). *Ethical action: Nurturing character in the classroom, EthEx Series, Book 4*. Notre Dame, IN: Alliance for Catholic Education Press.

Narvaez, D., & Bock, T. (2009). *Ethical judgment: Nurturing character in the classroom, EthEx Series, Book 2*. Notre Dame, IN: Alliance for Catholic Education Press.

Narvaez, D., Bock, T., & Endicott, L. (2003). Who should I become? Citizenship, goodness, moral flourishing, and ethical expertise. In W. Veugelers & F. Oser (Eds.), *Teaching in moral and democratic education*. Bern: P. Lang.

Narvaez, D., & Endicott, L. (2009). *Ethical sensitivity: Nurturing character in the classroom, EthEx Series, Book 1*. Notre Dame, IN: Alliance for Catholic Education Press.

Narvaez, D., & Lies, J. (2009). *Ethical motivation: Nurturing character in the classroom, EthEx Series, Book 3*. Notre Dame, IN: Alliance for Catholic Education Press.

Narvaez, D., Mitchell, C., Endicott, L., & Bock, T. (1999). *Nurturing character in the middle school classroom: A guidebook for teachers*. St. Paul, MN: Department of Children, Families, and Learning.

Neisser, U. (1967). *Cognitive psychology*. New York: Appleton-Century-Crofts.

Novick, L. R. (1988). Analogical transfer, problem similarity, and expertise. *Journal of Experimental Psychology: Learning, Memory, & Cognition, 14*(3), 510-520.

Piaget, J. (1952). *The origin of intelligence in children*. New York: International University Press.

Piaget, J. (1965*). The moral judgment of the child* (M. Gabain, Trans.). New York: Free Press. (Original work published 1932)

Piaget, J. (1970). *Genetic epistemology* (E. Duckworth, Trans.). New York: Columbia University Press.

Plato. (1987). *The republic*. London: Penguin.

Rogoff, B., Baker-Sennett, J., Lacasa, P., & Goldsmith, D. (1995). Development through participation in sociocultural activity. *Cultural Practices as Contexts for Development: New Directions for Child and Adolescent Development, 67*, 45-64.

Sternberg, R. (1998). Abilities are forms of developing expertise. *Educational Researcher, 3*, 22-35.

Sternberg, R. (1999). Intelligence as developing expertise. *Contemporary Educational Psychology, 24*(4), 359-375.

Preface

The *Nurturing Character in the Classroom, EthEx Series* materials were developed under the auspices of the Minnesota Community Voices and Character Education project (grant# R215V980001 from the U. S. Department of Education Office of Educational Research and Improvement to the Minnesota Department of Children, Families and Learning during 1998-2002).

The *Nurturing Character in the Classroom, EthEx Series* materials were developed in collaboration with teachers across the state of Minnesota and were tested throughout the project by volunteer teams of educators. **For a report of the final-year evaluation, see Narvaez, Bock, Endicott, and Lies (2004).**

EthEx refers to the lifelong development of ethical skills toward expertise (**eth**ical **ex**pertise) in many domains and situations. The four EthEx books (sensitivity, judgment, motivation, action) suggest skills and subskills required for virtuous life. The books also lay out how to teach them through four levels of expertise development.

EthEx is incorporated into the **Integrative Ethical Education** model (Narvaez, 2006, 2007, 2008, in press). The Integrative Ethical Education model has five steps for educators including (along with EthEx) the importance of a caring relationship with each student, a supportive climate (for achievement and character), student self-regulation for character and achievement, and restoring community networks and support.

These booklets were developed for the middle school level (ages 11-15), but elementary and high school teachers have used them successfully as well.

For **staff development** in your school, please contact Darcia Narvaez at the University of Notre Dame, Department of Psychology (dnarvaez@nd.edu). For questions or other materials, also contact Dr. Narvaez.

References

Narvaez, D. (2006). Integrative ethical education. In M. Killen & J. Smetana (Eds.), *Handbook of moral development* (pp. 703-733). Mahwah, NJ: Erlbaum.

Narvaez, D. (2007). How cognitive and neurobiological sciences inform values education for creatures like us. In D. Aspin & J. Chapman (Eds.), *Values education and lifelong learning: Philosophy, policy, practices* (pp. 127-159). Dordrecht, The Netherlands: Springer Press International.

Narvaez, D. (2008). Human flourishing and moral development: Cognitive science and neurobiological perspectives on virtue development. In L. Nucci & D. Narvaez (Eds.), *Handbook of moral and character education* (pp. 310-327). New York: Routledge.

Narvaez, D. (in press). *Moral development: A pragmatic approach to fostering engagement and imagination.*

Narvaez, D., Bock, T., Endicott, L., & Lies, J. (2004). Minnesota's voices and character education project. *Journal of Research in Character Education, 2,* 89-112.

Acknowledgments

Thanks to former University of Minnesota Team Members and affiliates whose ideas or efforts were influential at one point or another in the development of materials: Christyan Mitchell, Jolynn Gardner, Ruth Schiller, and Laura Staples.

Thanks to Connie Anderson, Minnesota Department of Children, Families and Learning, for her wisdom and leadership throughout the Community Voices and Character Education Project.

Special thanks to our school-based collaborators from across the state of Minnesota who kept us focused on what really works and what really helps the classroom teacher.

Introduction
to the
Ethical Expertise Model
(EthEx)

Purpose and Goals of the EthEx Model

At the beginning of the 21st century, children are less likely to spend time under adult supervision than they were in the past. As a result, children's ethical education has become haphazard, and subject to strong influence from popular media. To help the development of children, we seek to assist educators develop curricula that teach character while simultaneously meeting regular academic requirements. We apply research-based theory to instruction for ethical development, using an expertise model of ethical behavior that is based on research and applied to ethics education.

The Four Guide Books for Teachers

We have created four books[1] that address the four main psychological processes involved in behaving ethically: Ethical Sensitivity, Ethical Judgment, Ethical Motivation, and Ethical Action. Each book provides suggestions for ways to work on the skills of the process within regular lessons. Each book links ethics education to regular academic requirements. The four books are designed to help teachers develop a conscious and conscientious approach to helping students build character.

Why Not a Curriculum?

There are several problems with set curricula. First, the lessons are written out of the context of the classroom for which they are designed to be used. Consequently, no pre-fabricated lesson is actually taught exactly as designed because the teacher must adapt it to the students and class at hand. Second, we have seen too many curricula used once or twice and set aside as other demands claim teacher attention. So, although a set curriculum may appear more useful to the teacher at the outset, in the end it can become "old" as the latest mandate takes precedence. Third, an outside, packaged curriculum is often not assimilated into the teacher's way of thinking about instruction. Hence, it may feel "alien" to the teacher, a feeling that is correspondingly felt by students. So we believe that the best way to change teaching over the long term is to help teachers modify what they already teach. We make suggestions for changes, but the teacher herself modifies lessons in ways that work for her and her students. We believe that teacher tailoring is an approach that can bring lasting change.

[1]These materials have been developed under the auspices of grant # R215V980001 from the U.S. Department of Education Office of Educational Research and Improvement.

Should Teachers Teach Values?
They already are

To educate a person in mind and not in morals is to educate a menace to society.
-Theodore Roosevelt

The United States at the beginning of the 21st century has reached a new pinnacle. There is more prosperity throughout the society than ever before. There are more equal rights across groups (e.g., males and females, minorities and majorities) than at any time in the history of the world. There are comforts U.S. citizens enjoy that are accessible only to the wealthy in many other nations of the world (e.g., clean water, sewage, inexpensive clothes, and food). Then why are children around the nation shooting their peers at school? Why do so many lament our public behavior and sense of community? Why do some argue that our social supports are the worst among industrialized countries of the world (e.g., no national day care, few national benefits for parents)? Why does the U.S. have a greater percentage of its citizens imprisoned than any other nation save Russia? Certainly there are multiple causes for these outcomes. Many people, however, are concerned about the cultural health of our nation.

What do you think of our nation's cultural health? Take, for example, current standards for public behavior—are they better or worse than in the past? What do you think of popular culture? Television shows use language, discuss topics, and show interactions that would not have been broached just a few years ago. For the sake of entertainment, committed couples allow themselves to be placed on "Temptation Island" in order to test how committed they really are. Is that all right? On the popular show "The Ozbournes" the parents fully use profanity. Does it matter? Professional athletes can be felons and still receive acclaim from fans and the news media. Should we care? Many have noted that citizens are increasingly impatient, self-absorbed, and rude in public. Have you noticed? Most notably, people are harming and killing others over traffic offenses (e.g., Road Rage Summit, Minneapolis, April 29, 1999).

Citizens of other industrialized nations are appalled by our culture and consider us a nation of self-indulgent adolescents:

> Americans are like children: noisy, curious, unable to keep a secret, not given to subtlety, and prone to misbehave in public. Once one accepts the American's basically adolescent nature, the rest of their culture falls into place and what at first seemed thoughtless and silly appears charming and energetic. (Faul, 1994, p. 5)

Do you agree? Do you believe that individuals in the United States overemphasize their rights with little thought for their responsibilities to others? Do they (we) overemphasize individualism at the expense of collective goals as communitarians contend (e.g., Bellah, Madsen, Sullivan, Swidler, & Tipton, 1985; Etzioni, 1994)? According to this perspective, everyone is rushing from one activity to another with little thought for neighbors. The patience that is learned from long-time interaction with neighbors is not being fostered. Instead, impatience with others seems the norm. Miss Manners concurs, believing that we have a civility crisis.

Consider today's families. At the dawn of the 21st century in the United States, it is normal for parents (supported by corresponding laws and social beliefs) to think of themselves as individuals first and family members second, making it easy to divorce a spouse even when there are children. Even as a single parent works hard to support the family (or both parents work to maintain a standard of living formerly supported by one income), many are unable to provide the support and supervision their children need (Steinberg, 1996). As a result, children are not getting enough adult attention. A third of them are depressed. Too many commit suicide. They turn to their peers for values, support, and goals.[2] Children spend more time with television, with all its contemporary crudities, than with their parents. Children's values are cultivated willy-nilly by their daily experience largely apart from adults. Some young people admire Eminem, a White rap singer whose songs are replete with the raping or killing of women (including his mother). In fact, some sociologists and philosophers have suggested that U.S. culture, in its fascination with killing, is a culture not only of violence but of death. Such are the values that children bring to school.

"So what?" you might say. "I try not to make judgments about the cultures of my students. I let the students make up their own minds. I don't teach values in my classroom." Really? Is any behavior acceptable in your room? If not, you are teaching values; you are indicating that some behaviors are better than others. Not hitting is better than hitting. Not cheating is better than cheating. On a daily basis, you decide which students or behaviors get rewarded and which get punished. Teachers make decisions about how "the benefits and burdens of living together are distributed" (Rest, 1986). Teachers decide how to manage the competition and cooperation that humans bring to social interactions. In short, teachers are teaching values all day long.

[2] Unlike most other industrialized nations, there are few social supports outside the home that are built into our system; it was designed to rely on the strength of the nuclear family and extended family. A high rate of single parenting, both parents working and the resultant guilt, lack of parenting skills, lack of extended family support, and a cultural milieu oriented to pleasure rather than self-sacrifice all contribute to the decline in communal satisfaction. Instead of child raising being shared across society, the schools are shouldering the many needs that growing (and neglected or abused) children have.

Teachers' Ethical Decisions

We urge teachers to be both conscious of and conscientious about the values they are teaching.

There are many morally-relevant situations in schools in which teachers make decisions that affect student welfare. Here are a few concrete examples of value teaching:

- When teachers **divide the class into groups**, they are conveying what should be noticed (e.g., gender) and what they value (e.g., cooperation, achievement). By doing this they reinforce what students should notice and value.
- When teachers **discipline** students, the students learn what behaviors are important in that classroom (or in the hallway, depending on where the disciplining takes place).
- The **school rules the teacher enforces (or doesn't enforce)** reveal how seriously the students should take rules in school and in general.
- The **standards a teacher applies** to behavior, homework, and attitudes are practiced (and learned) by the students in the classroom.
- **The way a classroom is structured physically** and the way the teacher sets up procedures (and which ones) demonstrate the values held by the teacher. For example, if the teacher wants to emphasize creativity he or she may have colorful decor, alternating seating arrangements, and may allow freedom of choice in selecting academic activities.
- **The teacher's communication style** (quiet and firm, or playful and easy going) can set the climate and convey expectations for behavior.
- Whether or not and how teachers **communicate with parents** show how parents are valued.
- **Grading policies** are another way that teachers distribute the benefits and burdens available in the classroom—does the teacher use norm-references or criterion-references or contract-based grading?
- **Curriculum content selection** can convey a high regard for one culture over another, one viewpoint over another. Whether or not teachers assign homework over religious holidays (and whose holidays) reveal the teacher's expectations and values.
- **The teacher's cultural assumptions** about the social context and his or her instinctive responses to students convey non-verbally who is valued and who is not. This may be one of the most important features of a classroom for a minority student whose success may be at risk.

In short, teachers teach values whether or not they realize it. We urge teachers to be both conscious and conscientious about the values they are teaching. Hence this book has goals for teacher development. As teachers develop curricula using our principles, they will learn the principles to use in their professional behavior. First, we will discuss the process of ethical behavior. Then we will discuss how to apply this knowledge in the classroom—for both curriculum and for general climate in the classroom. Based on these materials, teachers will be able to design activities and a classroom that promote ethical behavior.

This is not to say that teachers currently are without guidance as to promoting an ethical classroom. Teachers have a code of ethics to which they subscribe when obtaining a license and a position. Notice the table from the National Education Association's Code of Ethics. These codes affect much of what teachers decide and do. Notice that the NEA code is not one of "doing no harm," but is proactive, that is, "doing good."

FROM THE CODE OF ETHICS OF THE EDUCATION PROFESSION
(National Education Association, 1975)

Principle 1: Commitment to the student.

In fulfillment to the student, the educator

1. Shall not unreasonably restrain the student from independent action in the pursuit of learning.
2. Shall not unreasonably deny the student access to varying points of view.
3. Shall not deliberately suppress or distort subject matter relevant to the student's progress.
4. Shall make reasonable effort to protect the student from conditions harmful to learning or to health and safety.
5. Shall not intentionally expose the student to embarrassment or disparagement.
6. Shall not on the basis of race, color, creed, sex, national origin, marital status, political or religious beliefs, family, social or cultural background, or sexual orientation, unfairly:
     a. Exclude any student from participation in any program;
     b. Deny benefits to any student;
     c. Grant any advantage to any student.

The NEA code requires teachers:

* to present more than one viewpoint,
* to present the full gamut of subject matter relevant to the student,
* to protect the student from harm.

These are actions that require conscious deliberation. For example, questions the teacher might consider are: What are multiple viewpoints on this topic? What content should be included? What harms students and how can I design an environment and classroom atmosphere that is least harmful? What if a student has a viewpoint that is legitimately harmful or wrong? If the teacher does not deliberately plan around these issues, chances are there will be only mainstream viewpoints presented, the subject matter will be narrow, and the student may have to tolerate insults and other harm from peers.

We believe that there is more to ethical education than even following a code of ethics. The code provides a minimal set of general guidelines. Promoting ethical behavior in students requires not only a deliberate effort but a theory for what ethical behavior entails. In character education programs across the country, it is not always clear what direction these efforts should take. That is the topic of the next section.

What Should Be Taught?
The Process Model of Ethical Behavior

When a curriculum claims to be educating for character, what should it mean? What are the aspects of ethics that should be addressed? As a framework for analysis, we use the process model of ethical behavior as described by Rest (1983) and advocated by Bebeau, Rest, and Narvaez (1999). The model includes ethical sensitivity, ethical judgment, ethical motivation, and ethical action. See the framework outlined below and described in the next section.

The Process Model of Ethical Behavior

ETHICAL SENSITIVITY
NOTICE!
Pick up on the cues related to
ethical decision making and behavior;
Interpret the situation according to who is involved,
what actions to take, and what possible reactions
and outcomes might ensue.

ETHICAL JUDGMENT
THINK!
Reason about the possible actions in the situation
and judge which action is most ethical.

ETHICAL MOTIVATION
AIM!
Prioritize the ethical action over other goals and needs
(either in the particular situation, or as a habit).

ETHICAL ACTION
ACT!
Implement the ethical action by knowing how to do so
and follow through despite hardship

How the Ethical Process Model Works

A kindergarten student in New York City dies midyear from longstanding child abuse at the hands of a parent. The community is shocked that the teacher and school did not prevent the untimely death.

The star of the boy's basketball team is flunking English. If he gets a failing grade, he won't be able to play on the team. Should the teacher give him a passing grade so that the team has a chance to win the championship and boost school morale?

An American Indian student won't look the teacher in the eye nor volunteer answers in class. How should the teacher respond?

From large effects to small, the ethical behavior of teachers—or the lack thereof—influences children's lives on a daily basis (e.g., Bergem, 1990; Goodlad, Soder, & Sirotnik, 1990). Decisions about grading and grouping; decisions about curriculum, instructional style, assessment; decisions about the allotment of time, care, and encouragement (which students, when, where, and how?)—all of these are ethical decisions the educator faces each day. How can teachers sort out the processes of ethical decision making?

First, one must know what ethical behavior looks like. When thinking about ethical behavior, it is often helpful to think of ethical failure. For example, albeit an extreme one, think of the teacher whose student dies from child abuse. How is it that the teacher did not take ethical action and intervene? There are many points at which failure might have occurred. First, the teacher would have to recognize the signs and symptoms of abuse, and have some empathic reaction to the child's circumstance. Having noticed and felt concern, the teacher would need to think about what action might be taken and what outcomes might occur. Then the teacher must reason about the choices and decide which action to take. (In order for ethical behavior to eventually occur, the teacher would need to select an ethical action). Next, the teacher would need to prioritize the chosen (ethical) action over other needs, motives, and goals. Finally, the teacher would need to know what steps to take to implement the decision, and persevere until the action was completed. It is apparent that there are a lot of places where things can go wrong. For example, the teacher may not see the signs or may make a bad judgment or may have other priorities or may not know what to do or may give up in frustration. In effect, ethical failure can stem from any one or more of these weaknesses.

Rest (1983) has asked: What psychological elements are involved in bringing about an ethical action? He has suggested that there are at least four psychological processes of ethical behavior that must occur in order for an ethical behavior to ensue. These four processes are:

(1) *Ethical Sensitivity:* Noticing the cues that indicate a moral situation is at hand. Identifying the persons who are interested in possible actions and outcomes and how the interested parties might respond to the range of possible actions and outcomes.

(2) *Ethical Judgment:* Making a decision about what is ethically right or ethically wrong in the situation.

(3) *Ethical Motivation:* Placing the ethical action choice at the top of one's priorities, over all other personal values at the moment.

(4) *Ethical Action:* Having the necessary ego strength and implementation skills to complete the action despite obstacles, opposition, and fatigue.

In an effort to make these processes clear, let us look at a specific situation in a classroom to which we will apply the processes. Let us imagine that Mr. Anderson has a classroom of children in which Abraham is hitting Maria. Now let us look at each of the processes in relation to this event.

Process 1: Ethical Sensitivity

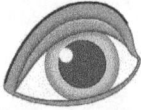

Picking up on the cues related to ethical decision making and ethical behavior. Interpreting the situation according to who is involved, what actions to take, what possible reactions and outcomes might ensue.

Teachers need to be able to detect and interpret environmental cues correctly in order for the other processes of ethical behavior to be initiated. For example, if Mr. Anderson completely fails to see Abraham hitting Maria, there will be no consideration of action choices or action taken. In order to perceive the action, such an occurrence must be salient because, for example, it is unusual. On the other hand, Mr. Anderson may not notice the hitting if it is a daily class-wide event, or if it is an agreed-upon sign of affection.

Ethical Sensitivity

Notice a problem (sensibilities)
What kinds of problems are salient to me, my family, my community, my affiliative groups?

State the situation (critical thinking)
What is the problem? How did the problem come about? How much time is there to make a decision? How does my community identify the problem? How do elders in my family identify the problem? How does my religion or family culture affect my perceptions?

State the interested parties (critical thinking)
Who are the people who will be affected by this decision (family, community, affiliative groups)? Who should be consulted in this decision? Who has faced this problem before? With whom could I talk about the problem?

Weigh the possible outcomes—short-term and long-term (creative thinking)
What are the possible consequences to me, my family/community/affiliative groups for each possible action? What are the possible reactions of these interested parties? What are the potential benefits for me, my family/community/affinity groups for each possible action? Who else might be affected? How will my choice affect the rest of the world now and in the future?

List all possible options (creative thinking)
How could the problem be solved? What are the choices I have for solving the problem? How would my community/family/cultural group solve the problem? What are the choices my family/cultural/community allow? Should I consider other options?

In intercultural/intersocial-class situations, cue misperception may take place, leading to improper action or no action at all. For example, a middle-class teacher in the U.S.A. may subconsciously perceive the downcast eyes of a Native American student in conversation with her as a sign of disrespect toward her authority. But in the student's own culture, the opposite is the case. However, out of ignorance the teacher may take an action to re-establish her authority, for example, punish the child. In contrast, a child may exhibit disrespectful behavior for his own sub-culture, such as severe slouching for some African-American communities.

However, this action is not really noticed since it is not considered out of the ordinary by the non-African-American teacher or interpreted as a threat to her authority (which it is intended to be) but is considered to be an acceptable expression of frustration on behalf of the student. In this case, the teacher interprets (subconsciously) the child's behavior as a personal freedom issue rather than the challenge to authority (a responsibility issue) that it is.

Ethical sensitivity includes subconscious processing which is often culturally based. As such, teachers need to become aware of their culturally-based expectations and to broaden their understanding of other cultural perspectives in order to circumvent misinterpretation of student behavior.

Not only is Mr. Anderson faced with many perceptual cues to sort through each day, he is also faced with countless situations in which he must make decisions with partial information. Before making a decision, he must interpret situations contextually, according to who is interested in the outcome, what actions and outcomes are possible and how the interested people might react to each. Many problems are much more complicated than in our example (e.g., whether or not to promote a student to the next grade). Here, it is obvious that hitting is generally wrong.

In our incident with Abraham and Maria, Mr. Anderson has noticed the action and finds it out of the ordinary and unacceptable. Now he must determine who is interested in the decision he makes about the incident—certainly Abraham and Maria would be interested, as well as their parents and families, the school administrator, not to speak of the other children in the classroom. Next, he thinks about the actions he could take in this situation and the likely outcomes and reactions of interested parties. For example, he might quickly think:

> *Well, I could stop what I am doing and verbally intervene in front of the whole class. Maybe that is not such a good idea because it would disrupt everyone's work. If Abraham does not stop, other children might notice and perhaps think that hitting was permissible. I could walk over there and physically intervene—grab Abraham's hand. That would stop it and still draw attention from the others— maybe they would learn something. Or, I could ignore it, since Abraham tends to do this when he gets excited—he means no harm. But how would Maria react to that? If I don't do something, Maria's parents might complain to the administrator.*

Ethical sensitivity involves attending to relevant events and mapping out possible actions and their effects. It includes a subtle interaction between both conscious and subconscious processing.

ETHICAL SENSITIVITY SKILLS
ES-1: Understanding Emotional Expression
ES-2: Taking the Perspective of Others
ES-3: Connecting to Others
ES-4: Responding to Diversity
ES-5: Controlling Social Bias
ES-6: Interpreting Situations
ES-7: Communicating Well

Process 2: Ethical Judgment

*Reasoning about the possible actions in the situation
and judging which action is most ethical.*

Following this exploration of possible actions and reactions, the ethical actor must decide on which course of action to take. Ethical judgment is the process of making a decision about which action of all the options is the most moral action. Lawrence Kohlberg (1984) defined different ways that people make decisions about how to get along with others (see the chart on p. 15). Whereas in ethical sensitivity, cultural differences are particularly important, in moral judgment, normative developmental trends in moral judgment are important. The types of moral reasoning Kohlberg found are developmental and have been identified in dozens of countries around the world. Although there are other types of criteria individuals use to make ethical decisions, Kohlberg's framework has extensive empirical research support. In addition, the vast majority of research shows no gender differences.

Ethical Judgment

Make a decision
What is the best action to take? What choice should I make? Why?

Ethical judgment concerns choosing the ethical action from the choices considered in the process of ethical sensitivity; this decision will be influenced by the ethical reasoning structures of the decision maker. In other words, Mr. Anderson selects the action that is the most ethical in the particular situation according to his level of ethical judgment development. In our scenario, Mr. Anderson may decide that, out of the choices we listed above, going over to Abraham and physically intervening is the most defensible ethical action:

It prevents further harm to Maria, and has ramifications for future behavior by Abraham and the rest of the class. It sends a clear signal both to Abraham and the rest of the class about how the students should NOT treat each other. I can use it as an opportunity to discuss the importance of following rules to keep order and safety in the classroom.

ETHICAL JUDGMENT SKILLS
EJ-1: Reasoning Generally
EJ-2: Reasoning Ethically
EJ-3: Understanding Ethical Problems

EJ-4: Using Codes and Identifying Judgment Criteria
EJ-5: Understanding Consequences
EJ-6: Reflecting on the Process and Outcome
EJ-7: Coping

SIX CONCEPTUAL STAGES ABOUT COOPERATION
AND THEIR CHARACTERISTICS
(From Rest, 1979)

PRECONVENTIONAL LEVEL

Stage 1: The ethicality of obedience: Do what you are told.
• Right and wrong are defined simply in terms of obedience to fixed rules.
• Punishment inevitably follows disobedience, and anyone who is punished must have been bad.
Example: Follow class rules to avoid detention.

Stage 2: The ethicality of instrumental egoism: Let's make a deal.
• An act is right if it serves an individual's desires and interests.
• One should obey the law only if it is prudent to do so.
• Cooperative interaction is based on simple exchange.
Example: Do chores to get allowance.

CONVENTIONAL LEVEL

Stage 3: The ethicality of interpersonal concordance: Be considerate, nice and kind, and you'll make friends.
• An act is good if it is based on a prosocial motive.
• Being ethical implies concern for the other's approval.
Example: Share your gum with the class and people will find you likeable.

Stage 4: The ethicality of law and duty to the social order: Everyone in society is obligated to and protected by the law.
• Right is defined by categorical rules, binding on all, that fix shared expectations, thereby providing a basis for social order.
• Values are derived from and subordinated to the social order and maintenance of law.
• Respect for delegated authority is part of one's obligations to society.
Example: Obey traffic lights because it's the law.

POSTCONVENTIONAL

Stage 5: The ethicality of consensus-building procedures: You are obligated by the arrangements that are agreed to by due process procedures.
• Ethical obligation derives from voluntary commitments of society's members to cooperate.
• Procedures exist for selecting laws that maximize welfare as discerned in the majority will.
• Basic rights are preconditions to social obligations.
Example: Obey traffic lights because they are designed to keep us all safe.

Stage 6: The ethicality of non-arbitrary social cooperation: How rational and impartial people would organize cooperation defines ethicality.
• Ethical judgments are ultimately justified by principles of ideal cooperation.
• Individuals each have an equal claim to benefit from the governing principles of cooperation.
Example: Everyone agrees that traffic lights keep us safe and so they will obey them for the common good.

Process 3: Ethical Motivation

*Prioritizing the ethical action over other goals and needs
(either in the particular situation, or as a habit).*

Following Mr. Anderson's decision about which action is most ethical, he must be motivated to prioritize that action, that is, be ethically motivated. Ethical motivation can be viewed in two ways, as situation-specific and as situation-general. Situation-general motivation concerns the day-to-day attitudes about getting along with others. It is a positive attitude towards ethical action that one maintains day to day. Blasi (1984) and Damon (1984) argue that self-concept has a great deal to do with ethical motivation generally, including attending to professional ethical codes. For instance, if one has a concept that one is an ethical person, one is more likely to prioritize ethical behaviors. Situation-specific ethical motivation concerns the prioritization of the ethical action choice in a particular situation. If all goes well, matching one's professional and personal priorities with possible actions results in ethical motivation, prioritizing the ethical action.

Ethical Motivation

Value identification
What are the values of my family/religion/culture/community? How should these values influence what is decided? How does each possible option fit with these values?

Prioritize the action
Am I willing to forego the benefits of NOT taking this best action?

Ethical motivation means that the person has placed the ethical course of action—which was selected in the process of ethical judgment— at the top of the list of action priorities. In other words, all other competing actions, values and concerns are set aside so that the ethical action can be completed. In other words, does a teacher put aside another priority at the moment, such as taking a break, in order to take an ethical action, such as stopping one student from insulting another? In our situation with Mr. Anderson, in order to continue along the route to completing an ethical action, he would have to put aside any other priority (such as teaching the lesson) and focus on performing the ethical action.

ETHICAL MOTIVATION SKILLS
EM-1: Respecting Others
EM-2: Cultivating Conscience
EM-3: Acting Responsibly
EM-4: Being a Community Member
EM-5: Finding Meaning in Life
EM-6: Valuing Traditions and Institutions
EM-7: Developing Ethical Identity and Integrity

*Implementing the ethical action by knowing how to do so
and following through despite hardship.*

Once Mr. Anderson has determined his priorities, he must complete the action and this requires ethical action. Ethical action involves two aspects: ego strength, the ability to persevere despite obstacles and opposition, and implementation skills, knowing what steps to take in order to complete the ethical action.

Ethical Action

Judge the feasibility of the chosen option
What is my attitude about taking this action? Do I believe it is possible for me to take this action? Do I believe that it is likely I will succeed?

Take action
What steps need to be taken to complete the action? Whose help do I need in my family/community/affiliative group? What back up plan do I have if this doesn't work?

Follow through
How do I help myself follow through on this action? How can others help me follow through? How do I resist giving up? How do I muster the courage to do it?

Reflect
What were the consequences of my decision? How did the decision affect me/my family/community/affiliative groups? Did the results turn out as I planned? In the future, should I change the decision or the decision process?

In our situation, Mr. Anderson might be very tired and have to draw up his strength and energize himself in order to take action. The implementation skills required in our scenario might include the manner of Mr. Anderson's intervention (e.g., severe and degrading reprimand versus a kind but firm reproach; or a culturally-sensitive approach that saves a student's 'face').

Let us consider another example. Perhaps a teacher knows that one of her students is smoking when he goes to the lavatory and she believes that it is best to stop him. Ethical action means that she has the action or fortitude to complete the ethical course of action. Many obstacles can arise to circumvent taking the ethical action. For example, if the student is 6 1/2 feet tall, she may feel physically threatened by the thought of confronting him and not even try. On the other hand, she may or may not know what steps to take to handle the situation. For example, to overcome fear for personal safety, she could ask another (bigger) teacher to help her or may inform the head of the school.

ETHICAL ACTION SKILLS
EA-1: Resolving Conflicts and Problems
EA-2: Asserting Respectfully
EA-3: Taking Initiative as a Leader
EA-4: Planning to Implement Decisions
EA-5: Cultivating Courage
EA-6: Persevering
EA-7: Working Hard

Need for All the Processes

These processes—ethical sensitivity, ethical judgment, ethical motivation, and ethical action—comprise the minimal amount of psychological processing that must occur for an ethical behavior to result. They are highly interdependent. That is, all the processes must be successfully completed before ethical behavior takes place. If one process fails, ethical action will not occur. For instance, if a teacher is highly sensitive to her students and environment but makes poor decisions (e.g., bargaining with students for their cooperation each day), poor outcomes may result. Or, a teacher may be sensitive to the situation, make a responsible ethical judgment, be highly motivated, but lack the backbone to follow through when a student challenges his action.

The processes also interact. That is, one may be so focused on one of the processes that it affects another process. For instance, the teacher who fears for her own safety or who values peace within the classroom may not challenge the students but try to keep them happy by not confronting any miscreant behaviors. Or, a teacher who is extremely tired and wanting to go home to rest may also be less sensitive to the needs of his students and miss cues that indicate ethical conflict.

Teaching Students Ethical Skills

The four-process model outlined here is helpful when thinking about designing instruction to promote ethical behavior. Like teachers, students face ethical dilemmas and situations each day. They have countless opportunities to demonstrate civic and ethical behavior. Their responses may be thoughtful and considerate or may be thoughtless and harmful to self and others. The teacher has a unique opportunity to help students nurture thoughtfulness and consideration of others. Our framework is intended to provide goals for teachers to do so. Our guide booklets suggest methods for reaching these goals during regular instruction.

We parcel each of the four processes into skills. The categorization of skills is not exhaustive but consists of skills that can be taught in a public school classroom. (There are other aspects of the processes that are either controversial or difficult to implement and assess in the public school classroom.) On the next page, we list the whole set of skills that are discussed in the guide booklets.

Ethical Behavior Skills for the Ethical Process Model

Activity Booklet 1: ETHICAL SENSITIVITY
ES-1: Understanding Emotional Expression
ES-2: Taking the Perspective of Others
ES-3: Connecting to Others
ES-4: Responding to Diversity
ES-5: Controlling Social Bias
ES-6: Interpreting Situations
ES-7: Communicating Well

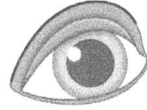

Activity Booklet 2: ETHICAL JUDGMENT
EJ-1: Reasoning Generally
EJ-2: Reasoning Ethically
EJ-3: Understanding Ethical Problems
EJ-4: Using Codes and Identifying Judgment Criteria
EJ-5: Understanding Consequences
EJ-6: Reflecting on the Process and Outcome
EJ-7: Coping

Activity Booklet 3: ETHICAL MOTIVATION
EM-1: Respecting Others
EM-2: Cultivating Conscience
EM-3: Acting Responsibly
EM-4: Being a Community Member
EM-5: Finding Meaning in Life
EM-6: Valuing Traditions and Institutions
EM-7: Developing Ethical Identity and Integrity

Activity Booklet 4: ETHICAL ACTION
EA-1: Resolving Conflicts and Problems
EA-2: Asserting Respectfully
EA-3: Taking Initiative as a Leader
EA-4: Planning to Implement Decisions
EA-5: Cultivating Courage
EA-6: Persevering
EA-7: Working Hard

How Should Character Be Taught?
Development Through Levels of Expertise

Each process of the Ethical Expertise Model is divided into several skills. The skills in each process include elements that we think are fundamental and have aspects that can be taught.

We present the skills in terms of expertise development. Think about how a young child learns to talk. First the child is exposed to sounds of all sorts, rather quickly learning the specialness of speech sounds in the environment. The child begins to make sounds, later to mimic and have mock conversations with a responsive caregiver. After many months, an actual word is spoken. From there, the child adds to his or her vocabulary little by little and then in floods. Think of how many hours a child has heard speech before age 2. Think of how much there is to learn yet after age 2. There are many phases of development in language acquisition and mastery. These phases (or levels) are movements toward expertise—toward the eloquence of an Eleanor Roosevelt or William F. Buckley, Jr. We use the notion of expertise in making recommendations for instruction.

Why Use an Expertise Approach?

> Billy has an IQ of 121 on a standardized individual intelligence test; Jimmy has an IQ of 94 on the same test. What do each of these scores, and the difference between them, mean? The ... best available answer to this question is quite different from the one that is conventionally offered—that the scores and the difference between them reflect not some largely inborn, relatively fixed ability construct, but rather a construct of developing expertise. I refer to the expertise that all of these assessments measure as developing rather than as developed because expertise is typically not at an end state but is in a process of continual development. (Sternberg, 1998, p. 11)

Current understanding of knowledge acquisition adopts the construct of novice-to-expert learning. According to this paradigm, individuals build their knowledge over time during the course of experience related to the knowledge domain. Robert Sternberg is a world-renown expert on human abilities and cognition who contends that abilities are developing expertise. Standardized tests measure how much expertise you've developed in a particular subject area or domain (and how much expertise you have at taking such tests).

In general, what do experts have that novices do not have?
Here is a list that Sternberg (1998) garners from research.
- Experts have large, rich, organized networks of concepts (schemas) containing a great deal of declarative knowledge about the domain
- Experts have well-organized, higher interconnected units of knowledge in the domain

What can experts do that novices cannot do?
Sternberg (1998) says that experts can:

- Develop sophisticated representations of domain problems based on structural similarities
- Work forward from given information to implement strategies for finding unknowns in problem solving
- Choose a strategy based on elaborate schemas for problem solving
- Use automated sequences of steps in problem solving
- Demonstrate highly efficient problem solving
- Accurately predict the difficulty of solving certain problems
- Carefully monitor their own problem-solving strategies and process
- Demonstrate high accuracy in reaching appropriate solutions to problems

The level of expertise described by Sternberg requires extensive study and deliberate practice. In primary and secondary schooling, there are many subjects to be covered and little time to spend on each one. Nevertheless, teachers can approach the subject matter as a domain of knowledge that novices can, over time, learn to master. Nurturing mastery of a domain is a lifelong endeavor. Teachers have a chance to help students develop the attitudes and motivation to monitor their own progress toward expertise.

How can novices develop expertise?
Sternberg (1998) suggests that novices should:

- Receive direct instruction to build a knowledge base (lecture, tutoring)
- Engage in actual problem solving
- Engage in role modeling of expert behavior
- Think about problems in the domain and how to solve them
- Receive rewards for successful solution of domain problems

For each skill in a process, we have condensed the complex acquisition of expertise into five skill levels (a larger number would be unmanageable). The purpose of the levels is to give teachers an idea of what students need for developing the given skill, knowledge, or attitude, or what kinds of behavior exhibit a certain level of expertise development. The levels refer to phases of development as both a process (ways to learn a skill) and a product (skills learned). Within each level are many sublevels and supplementary skills that we have not attempted to name. Instead, we use terms that point to the broad processes of building expertise in the domain. The levels are cumulative, that is, each level builds on the previous level. Further, within each skill are many domains. To develop new skills in a domain, the individual circles back through the levels to develop expertise.

Novice-expert differences in the skill categories

Some skill categories are learned from infancy for most people, requiring little conscious effort. For example, *Reading and Expressing Emotion* comes about naturally as a part of learning to get along with others. However, not everyone learns these skills, or learns them well, and few learn them across cultural contexts. Therefore, we include these 'naturally-acquired' skills as areas for all to expand cross-culturally and for some to learn explicitly.

Other skill categories are not learned as a matter of course during childhood. Instead they require concentrated effort. For example, *Controlling Social Bias* does not come naturally to any human or human group. We include these 'studied' skills because they are critical for ethical behavior.

Breaking down the skill category

Although we have parsed the processes into skill categories, the skill categories themselves can be broken down further into sub-skills. <u>We encourage you and your team to do this as much as possible.</u> When you do this, consider what a novice (someone who knows nothing or very little) would need to learn.

On the next page is a brief description of each level of expertise.

Levels of Expertise of an Ethical Behavior Skill

LEVEL 1: IMMERSION IN EXAMPLES AND OPPORTUNITIES
Attend to the big picture, Learn to recognize basic patterns

The teacher plunges students into multiple, engaging activities. Students learn to recognize broad patterns in the domain (identification knowledge). They develop gradual awareness and recognition of elements in the domain.

LEVEL 2: ATTENTION TO FACTS AND SKILLS
Focus on detail and prototypical examples, Build knowledge

The teacher focuses the student's attention on the elemental concepts in the domain in order to build elaboration knowledge. Skills are gradually acquired through motivated, focused attention.

LEVEL 3: PRACTICE PROCEDURES
Set goals, Plan steps of problem solving, Practice skills

The teacher coaches the student and allows the student to try out many skills and ideas throughout the domain to build an understanding of how these relate and how best to solve problems in the domain (planning knowledge). Skills are developed through practice and exploration

LEVEL 4: INTEGRATE KNOWLEDGE AND PROCEDURES
Execute plans, Solve problems

The student finds numerous mentors and/or seeks out information to continue building concepts and skills. There is a gradual systematic integration and application of skills across many situations. The student learns how to take the steps in solving complex domain problems (execution knowledge).

Who Decides Which Values to Teach?
The community

We have presented a set of ethical skills selected according to what enables a person to get along ethically with others and to thrive as a human being. The skills are to be taught developmentally, helping students build expertise. But what do the ethical skills actually look like? For example, what does "respecting others" look like? If one were to travel around the world, the answer would vary. While respect itself is a value worldwide, each community has its own understanding of how it should look. For example, to show respect in some cultures, one speaks quietly and demurely with little eye contact. In other cultures, respect involves looking others in the eye and expressing one's opinions openly. Likewise, "communicating well" or "identifying consequences" can vary across communities. In other words, while in its essence an ethical skill is the same across contexts, it may look different. In the EthEx Model, students learn the different ways a skill appears in their community.

The EthEx Model project emphasizes the importance of embedding the skill categories in community cultural contexts. We encourage communities to be involved in the specific aspects of creating a curriculum for skill development. We hope that the actual day-to-day practice of the skills be determined on site, in the community. Students can gather information about the skill from the community (parents, elders) and bring back that information to the classroom. The teacher can tailor the classroom work to the local understanding of the skill. If there are many interpretations of the skills because of diverse families, this diversity is brought into the classroom by the students themselves.

The goal of any character education program is to build good community members, for it is in communities that students express their values, make ethical decisions, and take ethical action. To be an effective community member in the United States, students need skills for democratic citizenship. These skills are included in the list of ethical skills.

What Is the Student's Role?
To decide his or her own character

The student is not a passive trainee in an EthEx classroom. Through classroom posters and bookmarks, each student is encouraged to think about the following questions: "Who should I be? What should I become?" As teachers approach each skill, these are the questions that should be raised. The teacher can ask students about each skill category, "How do you want to be known?— as [a good communicator, a problem solver, a leader]?" Sometimes the teacher has to identify a particular adult that the student trusts and ask, "What would [so and so] want you to be?" Every day, students should feel empowered with the knowledge that they are creating their own characters with the decisions they make and the actions they take.

The EthEx Model includes both **skills for personal development** and **skills for getting along with others**. All skills are necessary for ethical personhood. The better one knows oneself, the better one can control and guide the self, and the better able one can interact respectfully with others. On the next page we list the skills and the primary focus of each one, which is either on the self or others.

Ethical Behavior Categories for Each Process

The categories are skills the individual needs to develop for reaching individual potential and skills for living a cooperative life with others.

Process Skills   Focus

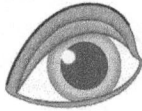

ETHICAL SENSITIVITY

ES-1: Understanding Emotional Expression	Self and Others
ES-2: Taking the Perspective of Others	Others
ES-3: Connecting to Others	Others
ES-4: Responding to Diversity	Self and Others
ES-5: Controlling Social Bias	Self
ES-6: Interpreting Situations	Self and Others
ES-7: Communicating Well	Self and Others

ETHICAL JUDGMENT

EJ-1: Reasoning Generally	Self
EJ-2: Reasoning Ethically	Self
EJ-3: Understanding Ethical Problems	Self and Others
EJ-4: Using Codes and Identifying Judgment Criteria	Self
EJ-5: Understanding Consequences	Self and Others
EJ-6: Reflecting on the Process and Outcome	Self and Others
EJ-7: Coping	Self

ETHICAL MOTIVATION

EM-1: Respecting Others	Others
EM-2: Cultivating Conscience	Self
EM-3: Acting Responsibly	Self and Others
EM-4: Being a Community Member	Others
EM-5: Finding Meaning in Life	Self and Others
EM-6: Valuing Traditions and Institutions	Self and Others
EM-7: Developing Ethical Identity and Integrity	Self

ETHICAL ACTION

EA-1: Resolving Conflicts and Problems	Self and Others
EA-2: Asserting Respectfully	Self and Others
EA-3: Taking Initiative as a Leader	Self and Others
EA-4: Planning to Implement Decisions	Self and Others
EA-5: Cultivating Courage	Self and Others
EA-6: Persevering	Self and Others
EA-7: Working Hard	Self

When Should Character Be Taught?
During regular instruction

EthEx stresses the importance of embedding character education into regular, academic, and standards-based instruction. We believe that character education should not stand alone but be incorporated into the entire spectrum of education for students. Regardless of the curriculum, teachers can always raise issues of ethics in lessons.

The second section of this book offers suggestions on how to integrate character development into regular academic instruction. The suggestions in this book are for only one of four processes. We hope you pick up the other three books in order to promote skill development in all processes and skills.

Characteristics of the EthEx Model

Provides a concrete view of ethical behavior
described in *What Should Be Taught?* section (pp. 9-19)

Focuses on novice-to-expert skill building
described in *How Should Character Be Taught?* section (pp. 20-23)

Addresses community cultural contexts
described in *Who Decides Which Values to Teach?* section (p. 24)

Empowers the student
described in *What Is the Student's Role?* section (pp. 25-26)

Embeds character education into regular instruction
described in *When Should Character Be Taught?* section (p. 27)

Ethical Sensitivity
How Ethical Sensitivity Skills Fit with Virtues

VIRTUE / SUBSKILL	ES-1 Emotional Expression	ES-2 Taking Persectives	ES-3 Connecting to Others	ES-4 Diversity	ES-5 Controlling Social Bias	ES-6 Interpret Situations	ES-7 Communic-ating Well
Altruism		*	*			*	
Citizenship		*			*	*	*
Civility			*				*
Commitment			*				
Compassion	*	*	*				
Cooperation			*	*	*		*
Courage							
Courtesy			*	*	*		*
Duty							
Fairness		*			*		
Faith			*				
Forbearance	*	*			*		
Foresight		*				*	
Forgiveness					*		
Friendship			*	*			*
Generosity		*	*				
Graciousness	*		*	*		*	*
Hard work							
Helpfulness		*	*			*	
Honesty	*		*				*
Honor							
Hopefulness						*	
Includes others		*	*	*	*	*	*
Justice		*			*		
Kindness	*		*				*
Lawfulness							
Loyalty			*	*			
Obedience							
Obligation							
Patience	*					*	*
Patriotism					*		
Persistence							
Personal Responsibility		*				*	
Politeness	*		*				*
Respect	*		*		*		*
Reverence			*				
Self-control	*						*
Self-sacrifice							
Social Responsibility		*		*	*	*	
Tolerance	*	*		*	*		
Trustworthiness			*				
Unselfishness		*					

Ethical Judgment
How Ethical Judgment Skills Fit with Virtues

VIRTUE / SUBSKILL	EJ-1 Reasoning Generally	EJ-2 Reasoning Ethically	EJ-3 Understand Problems	EJ-4 Using Codes	EJ-5 Conse-quences	EJ-6 Reflecting	EJ-7 Coping
Altruism		*		*		*	
Citizenship		*	*	*		*	
Civility		*		*		*	
Commitment		*		*	*	*	*
Compassion		*	*	*		*	
Cooperation		*				*	
Courage							
Courtesy		*		*		*	
Duty		*		*		*	
Faith		*		*		*	*
Fairness		*	*	*		*	
Forgiveness				*		*	
Friendship		*		*			
Forbearance		*		*		*	*
Foresight	*	*		*			
Generosity		*		*		*	
Graciousness				*			*
Hard work	*	*					
Helpfulness		*		*		*	
Honor		*		*		*	
Honesty		*		*		*	
Hopefulness							*
Includes others		*		*		*	
Justice		*	*	*		*	
Kindness		*		*		*	
Lawfulness		*	*	*		*	
Loyalty		*		*		*	
Obedience		*		*		*	
Obligation		*	*	*		*	
Patience	*				*		*
Patriotism		*		*		*	
Persistence	*						
Politeness				*			
Respect		*		*		*	*
Reverence		*		*		*	*
Personal Responsibility	*	*	*	*		*	
Social Responsibility		*	*	*	*	*	
Self-control					*		*
Self-sacrifice		*				*	
Tolerance		*		*		*	*
Trustworthiness							*
Unselfishness		*		*		*	

Ethical Motivation
How Ethical Motivation Skills Fit with Virtues

VIRTUE \ SUBSKILL	EM-1 Respecting Others	EM-2 Cultivating Conscience	EM-3 Acting Responsibly	EM-4 Community Member	EM-5 Finding Meaning	EM-6 Valuing Traditions	EM-7 Ethical Identity
Altruism				*	*		*
Citizenship	*	*	*	*		*	
Civility	*	*					*
Commitment		*	*	*	*	*	*
Compassion	*			*	*		*
Cooperation	*	*	*	*	*	*	
Courage		*		*	*		*
Courtesy	*						
Duty	*	*	*			*	
Faith				*	*		*
Fairness				*		*	
Forgiveness	*				*		
Friendship	*						
Forbearance	*	*		*			
Foresight	*		*		*	*	*
Generosity				*			*
Graciousness	*			*			
Hard work			*	*		*	
Helpfulness	*		*	*			
Honor		*	*		*	*	*
Honesty	*	*					
Hopefulness	*		*	*	*	*	*
Includes others	*			*		*	
Justice						*	
Kindness	*			*			*
Lawfulness		*	*			*	*
Loyalty		*	*			*	*
Obedience		*					
Obligation		*	*	*			
Patience	*		*	*	*	*	
Patriotism						*	
Persistence			*		*	*	*
Politeness	*			*			
Respect	*	*	*	*	*	*	*
Reverence	*	*	*	*	*	*	
Personal Responsibility	*	*	*			*	*
Social Responsibility	*		*	*		*	*
Self-control	*	*	*	*	*		*
Self-sacrifice		*		*			*
Tolerance	*	*	*	*		*	
Trustworthiness		*		*			*
Unselfishness	*	*	*	*	*		*

Ethical Action
How Ethical Action Skills Fit with Virtues

VIRTUE / SUBSKILL	EA-1 Resolving Conflicts	EA-2 Assertive-ness	EA-3 Initiative as Leader	EA-4 Planning	EA-5 Cultivating Courage	EA-6 Persevering	EA-7 Working Hard
Altruism			*		*	*	
Citizenship	*		*	*	*	*	*
Civility	*	*				*	
Commitment	*	*	*	*	*	*	*
Compassion		*	*	*	*		*
Cooperation	*	*	*	*			*
Courage		*	*		*		
Courtesy	*	*					
Duty	*		*	*	*	*	*
Fairness	*				*		
Faith			*	*	*		*
Forbearance	*	*	*		*	*	*
Foresight	*	*	*				*
Forgiveness							
Friendship	*			*			
Generosity			*		*		
Graciousness							
Hard work		*	*	*	*	*	*
Helpfulness			*		*	*	*
Honesty		*	*	*			
Honor	*		*	*	*		*
Hopefulness	*	*	*				
Includes others	*		*	*			
Justice	*			*	*		*
Kindness							
Lawfulness			*	*			*
Loyalty			*	*			*
Obedience							*
Obligation	*		*	*			*
Patience	*	*	*			*	*
Patriotism			*	*	*		
Persistence	*	*	*		*	*	*
Personal Responsibility	*		*		*	*	*
Politeness		*		*			
Respect	*	*	*	*			
Reverence			*	*			
Self-control	*	*	*	*		*	*
Self-sacrifice			*		*	*	
Social Responsibility	*		*		*	*	*
Tolerance	*	*	*				
Trustworthiness		*	*				
Unselfishness	*		*	*	*		

References

Bebeau, M., Rest, J. R., & Narvaez, D. (1999). Beyond the promise: A framework for research in moral education. *Educational Researcher, 28*(4), 18-26.

Bellah, R., Madsen, R., Sullivan, W., Swidler, A., & Tipton, S. (1985). *Habits of the heart: Individualism and commitment in American life*. Berkeley: University of California Press.

Bergem, T. (1990). The teacher as moral agent. *Journal of Ethical Education, 19*(2), 88-100.

Blasi, A. (1984). Moral identity: Its role in moral functioning. In W. M. Kurtines & J. L. Gewirtz (Eds.), *Morality, moral behavior, and moral development* (pp. 128-139). New York: Wiley-Interscience.

Damon, W. (1984). Self-understanding and moral development from childhood to adolescence. In W. M. Kurtines & J. L. Gewirtz (Eds.), *Morality, moral behavior, and moral development* (pp. 109-127). New York: Wiley-Interscience.

Etzioni, A. (1994). *The spirit of community: The reinvention of American society*. New York: Simon & Schuster.

Faul, S. (1994). *Xenophobe's guide to the Americans*. London: Ravette.

Goodlad, J., Soder, R., & Sirotnik, K. (1990). *The moral dimensions of teaching*. San Francisco: Jossey-Bass.

Kohlberg, L. (1984). *The psychology of moral development*. New York: Harper & Row.

National Education Association. (1975). *Code of ethics of the education profession*. Retrieved February 5, 2009, from http://ethics.iit.edu/codes/coe/nat.edu.assoc.1975.html

Rest, J. R. (1979). *Development in judging moral issues*. Minneapolis: University of Minnesota Press.

Rest, J. R. (1983). Morality. In P. Mussen (Series Ed.), J. Flavell & E. Markham, (Volume Eds.), *Manual of child psychology: Vol. 3, Cognitive development* (pp. 556-269). New York: Wiley.

Rest, J. R. (1986). *Moral development: Advances in research and theory*. New York: Praeger.

Steinberg, L. (1996). *Beyond the classroom: Why school reform failed and what parents need to do*. New York: Simon and Schuster.

Sternberg, R. (1998). Abilities are forms of developing expertise. *Educational Researcher, 3*, 22-35.

Nurturing Ethical Judgment

Organization of Ethical Judgment Booklet

Overview Pages
Ethical Action skills and subskills

Skill Sections (7 skill sections in all—the *"meat"* of the booklet)
Skill Overview (see sample page below)
Subskills (see sample pages on p. 37)
>   Activities
>   Assessment hints
>   Climate suggestions

Appendix
Guide for Lesson Planning
'Linking to the Community' Worksheet
Rubric Examples
Special Activities
Resources
Linking EA Skills to Search Institute Assets
References

Skill Overview Page

Skill Title

Persevering

Ethical Action 6

WHAT the skill is

WHAT
Perseverance enables individuals to complete actions that are important to them and others. Without it, many ethical actions would fail at the sight of the first obstacle or difficulty.

WHY the skill is important

WHY
Perseverance is important for the completion of an ethical action. Children can be successfully instructed to 'talk to themselves' about not doing something, and instructed on how to distract themselves from unwanted behavior. A form of self-talk to complete a task can be a useful technique to help one find the ego strength to complete an ethical action—at any age.

EA-6 Developing Perseverance: Overview

Skill Name: Subskill Name
Side Header

SUBSKILLS list

SUBSKILLS OVERVIEW
Be steadfast
Overcome obstacles
Build competence

Ethical Judgment Overview

Subskill Activities Page

Skill & Subskill NAME

Expert Example

Subskill Activities by Level of Expertise
(4 levels total, usually spans 2-4 pages per subskill)

Persevering by Building Competence

Expert

Christopher Reeves (who played Superman in the movies) had an equestrian accident that left him a quadriplegic. He could have given up in life and stayed home quietly, but he became a spokesman for those with spinal injuries, traveling to speak about the importance of research in spinal injuries.

Ideas for Developing Skills

Level 1: Immersion in Examples and Opportunities
Attend to the big picture, Learn to recognize basic patterns

Study self-efficacy. Discuss how, for a particular field, small successes give a person confidence to keep trying and try harder things. Find examples in literature, television and movies, or in a particular subject area. ★

Level 2: Attention to Facts and Skills
Focus on detail and prototypical examples, Build knowledge

Self-talk. Find examples of and discuss how to 'cheerlead' for yourself in different situations. What behaviors help you do your best and reach excellence? (1) Students discuss self-talk and behaviors that help one persevere. (2) Students interview older students or adults about general behaviors. (3) Students interview adults in roles they admire or strive for in a particular field. ★

Level 3: Practice Procedures
Set goals, Plan steps of problem solving, Practice skills

Examples of pushing oneself in helping others. Students interview elders about their personal experiences of (1) how they persevered in trying to help others; (2) how they persevered in working towards a goal that helped humanity.

Level 4: Integrate Knowledge and Procedures
Execute Plans, Solve Problems

Self-help. Have students practice ways to coach oneself to reach excellence in skills like these for a particular subject area. Persistence in mental and physical [...] eting tasks without

EA-6 Developing Perseverance: Build competence

Assessment Hints

Build competence

Use multiple-choice, true-false, short answer, or essay tests to assess student's knowledge of strategies to push oneself.

Have students write reports, based on observations or interviews, of what they learned about pushing oneself.

Skill Name:
Subskill Name
Side Header

Hints for Assessment

Skill Climate Page

Create a Climate to Persevere

Regularly discuss the importance of finishing a task, as a group or individual.

Regularly point out what would happen if people did not persevere until a job was done (e.g., the highway, a bridge, your house, your car) and how it would affect people around them.

Discuss the importance of persevering in meeting your responsibilities to others.

Sample Student Self Monitoring
Persevering

Be steadfast
I wait to reward myself until I've finished my work.
I don't wait until the last minute to do my work.
I lose control when I am angry. (NOT)
I control my feelings of anger.
I resist my impulses to disobey rules.

EA-6 Developing Perseverance: Climate

What you need to know for success in school

1. That attitudes affect behavior
2. That what you believe/think about affects your behavior
3. That you have some control over your attitudes
4. That learning anything requires commitment (decision to put your energies into a task)

Suggestions for Creating a Climate to Develop Skill

Sample Self-Monitoring Questions for Student

Selections to Post in the Classroom
for Developing Skill

Ethical Judgment Overview

Ethical Processes & Skills

with Ethical Judgment Subskills

Activity Booklet 1: ETHICAL SENSITIVITY
ES-1 Understanding Emotional Expression
ES-2 Taking the Perspective of Others
ES-3 Connecting to Others
ES-4 Responding to Diversity
ES-5 Controlling Social Bias
ES-6 Interpreting Situations
ES-7 Communicating Well

Activity Booklet 3: ETHICAL MOTIVATION
EM-1 Respecting Others
EM-2 Cultivating Conscience
EM-3 Acting Responsibly
EM-4 Being a Community Member
EM-5 Finding Meaning in Life
EM-6 Valuing Traditions and Institutions
EM-7 Developing Ethical Identity and Integrity

Activity Booklet 4: ETHICAL ACTION
EA-1 Resolving Conflicts and Problems
EA-2 Asserting Respectfully
EA-3 Taking Initiative as a Leader
EA-4 Planning to Implement Decisions
EA-5 Cultivating Courage
EA-6 Persevering
EA-7 Working Hard

Activity Booklet 2: ETHICAL JUDGMENT

EJ-1 Reasoning Generally
Reasoning objectively
Using sound reasoning
Avoiding reasoning pitfalls

EJ-2 Reasoning Ethically
Judging perspectives
Reasoning about standards and ideals
Reasoning about actions and outcomes

EJ-3 Understanding Ethical Problems
Gathering information
Categorizing problem types
Analyzing ethical problems

EJ-4 Using Codes and Identifying Judgment Criteria
Characterizing codes
Discerning code application
Judging code validity

EJ-5 Understanding Consequences
Attending to consequences
Predicting consequences
Responding to consequences

EJ-6 Reflecting on the Process and Outcome
Reasoning about means and ends
Making right choices
Monitoring one's reasoning

EJ-7 Coping
Applying positive reasoning
Managing disappointment and failure
Developing resilience

Ethical Judgment

Ethical judgment involves reasoning about the possible actions in the situation and judging which action is most ethical. This component is influenced by Ethical Sensitivity and Motivation.

Outline of Skills

EJ-1: REASONING GENERALLY

Reasoning is a type of thinking that helps a person draw a conclusion based on a particular set of information (Overton, 1990). A reasonable conclusion is not random but is consistent with the information at hand. Flawed reasoning is used to support many prejudices and harmful actions. A good problem solver must be aware of the weaknesses in human reasoning and learn skills to counteract these pitfalls.

EJ-2: REASONING ETHICALLY

Students make judgments and decisions every day about how to get along with others. Students use ethical reasoning to make each and every one of these decisions. In using ethical reasoning, they think about what codes, rules, laws, or ideals a person should be following, which is the most fair, just, kind, dutiful action and what outcomes a decision may bring about.

EJ-3: UNDERSTANDING ETHICAL PROBLEMS

Understanding problems is one of the first steps in any problem-solving and decision-making process. It is a step that students tend to ignore. To fully understand a problem, regardless of the subject area, a person must correctly define the problem and determine what information is important and what is irrelevant. The problem solver gathers the information needed from credible sources. The problem solver organizes the important information in order to generate options and strategies for solving the problem.

EJ-4: USING CODES AND IDENTIFYING JUDGMENT CRITERIA

Codes are what we know and use to act respectfully and responsibly in different domains or contexts. The different sources of codes include explicit and implicit rules and laws and ethical standards, which may vary from one context to the next. Contexts may be more local, such as school, family, and work, or broader, such as national and international.

EJ-5: UNDERSTANDING CONSEQUENCES

Understanding consequences involves understanding the relationships between events and their consequences and then using that understanding to predict the possible consequences of actions being considered. It is important to be able to think about both short-term and long-term consequences, as well considering all the people who may be affected by an action. We need to be prepared for unforeseen consequences. We must practice and refine creative responses.

EJ-6: REFLECTING ON THE PROCESS AND OUTCOME

Reflection is an important metacognitive (or thinking about thinking) skill. It consists of examining one's thinking processes and outcomes. For students to consistently make good ethical decisions, they must reflect on both their *judgment process* and their *resulting decision*. Making right choices is complicated. To hone our choices into right choices, we must reflect on all that we do and orient our minds to do the right thing.

EJ-7: COPING

Resiliency is a set of skills, behaviors and attitudes that allow a person beset by high risk factors to survive and to thrive in the face of adversity. Low coping skills leave one susceptible to risk behaviors like substance abuse, behavior problems and low achievement. Cognitive coping skills include thinking positively about others, having hope for a satisfying future, finding the silver lining in most experiences, and having positive perseverance under adverse conditions.

Ethical Judgment

WHAT
Ethical judgment is reasoning about the possible actions in a given situation and judging which action is most ethical. A person making an ethical judgment uses reason to decide what the best solution or decision is in a problem. He or she contemplates such questions as "What is the best action to take?" and "Why is this particular action the best to take in this situation?"

WHY
Ethical judgment is a critical piece in the decision-making process. To make a good, sound decision or effectively solve a problem, a person must have some basic cognitive skills that enable them to thoroughly and systematically complete the decision-making process. These basic cognitive skills include understanding what the ethical problem is, knowing what codes can be applied to the situation, using reasoning to determine what the best decision is, reflecting on the situation to make sure that the best decision has been made, and planning how to implement the decision and judging whether the decision brought about good results.

ROLE OF TEACHER/ADULT
To help students develop ethical judgment skills, adults can explain the reasons behind their ethical decisions. They can also explain to students what the ethical problem is, reflect aloud on their decision, and explain their plans as to how the decision should be implemented. Adults can provide opportunities for students to make their own decisions and afterwards discuss the decision and how it was made.

TACKLING EXCUSES AND HANGUPS

Sometimes students will resist learning or taking action, giving excuses like the following. We offer suggestions about how to counteract these attitudes.

'Why should I bother about them?' (sense of superiority)
Discuss this as a general human bias that one must consciously control.

'Yup, I was right about those homeless people. They're just lazy.'
Discuss the human tendency to look only for confirming evidence of personal bias. Work on perspective-taking.

'I couldn't help it. I was so mad.'
Discuss or demonstrate the benefits of giving emotions a "cooling down period" and being objective.

'It's not my problem.'
Discuss human relatedness (ES-3) and ethical responsibility (EM-4).

'That looks/tastes/smells weird!'
Work on reducing fear of the unknown and difference. Discuss the realistic risks and benefits of learning about something new.

'It's just a TV show. I know it's not real.'
Discuss the harm of desensitization to violence and objectification of people.

'The consequences are too far in the future to concern me.' (This is especially pertinent to young people's attitudes toward drugs, alcohol.) Bring in guest speakers who had these thoughts/attitudes and then experienced the "far off" consequences. Encourage students to discuss issues with the speaker.

'The possible consequences will never happen to me.' (e.g., getting pregnant, being arrested for vandalism, other crimes.) Bring in guest speakers who had these thoughts/attitudes and then experienced the "unrealistic" consequences. Encourage students to discuss issues with the speaker.

'The possible consequences will never happen to him/her/them.'
Bring in guest speakers who had these thoughts/attitudes and then witnessed the "improbable" consequences occurring to another (e.g., killing a friend or stranger by driving drunk). Encourage students to discuss issues with the speaker and ask many questions.

'I have no choice—my friends are making me do this.'
Have students practice assertiveness skills: (1) Describe the situation that is upsetting, without blaming or getting emotional. (2) Tell other person your feelings. (3) Tell other person what you want him/her to change. (4) Tell other person how the change would make you feel.

'It's not my fault—person X is who you should blame!'
Counter with techniques to foster feelings of responsibility/accountability for one's own actions: (1) Discipline with immediate consequences and a given reason. (2) Help parents with discipline plans that include giving reasons to students when disciplined. (3) Discuss related dilemmas with slight variations.

'I can't change this situation so I won't try.'
Counter with inspirational examples of how others make a difference (e.g., Rosa Parks, or a local community member who has made a difference). Discuss how the student is more similar than different to this person. Emphasize how the student can make a difference.

'This situation is none of my concern.' (e.g., witnessing a fight or a crime)
Counter with citizenship activities, discussing the importance of concern for others in the community and outside of the community. Discuss the purpose of citizenship and its related responsibilities. Study exemplars of good citizenship.

'There's no time to think of other alternatives!'
Discuss (1) human tendencies to lose control (and do harm) when emotions are high, and (2) the importance of carefully and systematically thinking through a dilemma or problem and decision so others and yourself will not be harmed in the immediate or distant future.

'Why should their well-being be my concern?' (lack of positive regard for life)
Encourage a more positive regard for life and discuss in class people who have a healthy regard for life.

'It's not my responsibility to save the world!' (not seeing the value of human existence)
Counter with a discussion of the interconnectedness of us all and our ethical obligations to each other.

'Why should I help them? Nobody's ever done anything for me!' (pessimistic attitude resulting from negative life experience) Discuss the importance of optimism, and of overcoming obstacles.

'It's their own fault that they're in this mess...not mine.' (lack of empathic understanding of others) Foster a discussion of those who are empathic and how to help another in distress.

'I've got other things planned...I don't have time to help!' (having immediate needs that are in opposition to caring for others) Discuss the importance weighing others' needs against our own, developing courtesy, meeting obligations and showing generosity.

'Being a citizen of the U.S.A. means freedom to do what I want.'
Counter with examination and discussion of various forms of citizenship. Discuss the purpose of citizenship and its related responsibilities.

'This is stuff that adults do.'
Discuss examples of the positive and meaningful impact of young people on the world (e.g., dot-com companies, altruistic group leadership, etc.).

'This is the stuff that people in x-group do.'
Give counter examples to sex-typing, group typing.

'Other people will take care of it.'
Discuss this as a general human bias.

'I don't want to look like a fool in front of my classmates.'
Discuss counter examples of young people being seen as assertive, taking action for others and standing out.

'I'm afraid that my classmates might get back at me.' (This may come up especially if the peers are involved in unethical or illegal activities.) Discuss choices of peers, role models and the consequences.

'I don't like people in that group.'
Discuss the changing nature of group membership and feeling 'outside.'

'I can't do it.'
Discuss this as an obstacle to overcome.

Ethical Judgment
How Ethical Judgment Skills Fit with Virtues

VIRTUE / SUBSKILL	EJ-1 Reasoning Generally	EJ-2 Reasoning Ethically	EJ-3 Understand Problems	EJ-4 Using Codes	EJ-5 Conse-quences	EJ-6 Reflecting	EJ-7 Coping
Altruism		*		*		*	
Citizenship		*	*	*		*	
Civility		*		*		*	
Commitment		*		*	*	*	*
Compassion		*	*	*		*	
Cooperation		*				*	
Courage							
Courtesy		*		*		*	
Duty		*		*		*	
Faith		*		*		*	*
Fairness		*	*	*		*	
Forgiveness				*		*	
Friendship		*		*			
Forbearance		*				*	*
Foresight	*	*		*			
Generosity		*		*		*	
Graciousness				*			*
Hard work	*	*					
Helpfulness		*		*		*	
Honor		*		*		*	
Honesty		*		*		*	
Hopefulness							*
Includes others		*		*		*	
Justice		*	*	*		*	
Kindness		*		*		*	
Lawfulness		*	*	*		*	
Loyalty		*		*		*	
Obedience		*		*		*	
Obligation		*	*	*		*	
Patience	*				*		*
Patriotism		*		*		*	
Persistence	*						
Politeness				*			
Respect		*		*		*	*
Reverence		*		*		*	*
Personal Responsibility	*	*	*	*		*	
Social Responsibility		*	*	*	*	*	
Self-control					*		*
Self-sacrifice		*				*	
Tolerance		*		*		*	*
Trustworthiness							*
Unselfishness		*		*		*	

Selections to Post in the Classroom
for Ethical Judgment

MAKING DECISIONS

- <u>Decisions should be judged</u> on the basis of how they are made (Wheeler & Janis, 1980).
- <u>Sound decisions</u> are those that consider all relevant aspects of the problem (Wheeler & Janis, 1980).
- <u>To make a good decision you have to believe</u>:
  1. the risks are serious
  2. you can find a solution
  3. there is enough time to make a good decision

Selections to Post in the Classroom
for Ethical Judgment

TIPS FOR MAKING DECISIONS

Identify problem and decision to be made
- Identify the core issues from an impartial perspective
- Identify one's personal goals and the goals and interests of others
- Raise multiple perspectives of the dilemma

Identify criteria
- Consider all consequences (both positive and negative) of all alternatives, especially how alternative may affect others (including individuals in both the in- and out-group)

Evaluating options
- Ask *WHY* and *HOW* about each alternative
- Compare alternatives by keeping track of them on a "personal balance sheet" that lists the alternatives along with pros, cons, social considerations, impact to others, feasibility, etc.

Making a decision
- Be deliberate and systematic in reasoning
- Distinguish good and poor arguments/reasoning
- Set aside time for contemplation

At any point in the decision-making process, ask other people for input and advice.

Ethical Judgment 1

Reasoning Generally
(Think skillfully)

WHAT

Reasoning is a type of thinking that helps a person draw a conclusion based on a particular set of information (Overton, 1990). A reasonable conclusion is not random but is consistent with the information at hand. Flawed reasoning is used to support many prejudices and harmful actions. A good problem solver must be aware of the weaknesses in human reasoning and learn skills to counteract these pitfalls.

WHY

Reasoning helps us improve how we do things (Calne, 1999) and how we treat one another. For example, reason stopped the practice of slavery worldwide. Reason challenges our human biases of preferring the familiar and discrediting those who are different, and it has generated knowledge to allow us to travel half way across the world in one day. It has helped us create vaccinations, irrigation systems, self-governance systems, and many more things that have improved the human condition. In today's complex societies, reasoning is *necessary* to effectively function and participate in multiple contexts.

Web Wise

http://www.eco-justice.org/Brochure.asp

United States Institute of Peace has readings and information about peace and the causes of prejudice and war: www.usip.org

SUBSKILLS OVERVIEW

1: Reasoning impartially
Thinking deliberately
Distinguishing facts from non-facts
Avoid: Exaggerating the advantages and disadvantages of an alternative
Avoid: Minimizing the drawbacks of an alternative
Avoid: Minimizing the advantages of other alternatives
Avoid: Denying possible negative consequences of an alternative

2: Using sound reasoning
Using logic
Having adequate support for conclusions
Evaluating the validity of a claim

3: Avoiding human reasoning pitfalls
(List of pitfalls on page 59)

Kinds of Reasoning

Though the ability to reason is often perceived to be (and certainly can be!) an abstract, highly complex skill, children begin to learn and use reasoning at an early age. For example, young children understand the use of "if... then..." conditional statements (Braine, 1990). More complex forms of reasoning, such as formal deductive reasoning, start to emerge at around 10-12 years of age (Overton, 1990). Below are examples of more complex forms of deductive and inductive reasoning.

Deductive Reasoning—making inferences from general propositions to particular propositions
Examples of different kinds of deductive reasoning:
- Scientific reasoning (scientific laws and principles are applied to particular observations)
  For example, Newton's observation that whenever one drops something, it tends to fall to the ground, which helped formulate the Law of Gravity.
- Mathematical reasoning (mathematical laws are applied to particular observations)
  For example, mathematical theory is used to predict how people will behave in noncooperative games (see John Nash's work on game theory)

Inductive Reasoning—making inferences from particular propositions to general propositions
Examples of different kinds of inductive reasoning:
- Pragmatic reasoning (based on knowledge of context)
  For example, when the temperature outdoors is 0 degrees, I reason that I should wear a coat
- Statistical reasoning (based on probability)
  For example, if I have to reason who is the taller of a couple, the husband or the wife, I will reason 'husband' because men tend to be taller than women.

Reasoning Generally by Reasoning Objectively

Creative and Expert Implementer Real-Life Example

Oliver Wendell Holmes was one of the great Supreme Court Justices of the 20th century. He was known for his objective examination of the facts and law. He was very opinionated about what a democracy should be; however, he always kept an open mind and believed in letting others have their say and opportunity. Justice Holmes had excellent reflection skills to keep his own ideas and philosophies in check while objectively listening to and examining others' ideas and opinions of the law.

Ideas for Developing Skills

Level 1: Immersion in Examples and Opportunities
Attend to the big picture, Learn to recognize basic patterns

Facts vs. non-facts in a subject area. One of the best rules for reasoning objectively is that, wherever possible, there must be independent confirmation of the facts. If there isn't an independent confirmation, anyone can argue that his or her viewpoint represents the facts. (1) Have students act out role plays on a topic relevant to your lesson. Ask other students to describe the role plays. Ask the class to determine what in the descriptions are facts and what are opinions. (2) Play a newscast about something familiar to the students or relevant to the subject matter being studied. Ask students to discern what aspects of the newscast are factual, half-truths, or opinions (e.g., UFO's, global warming). (3) Select a set of statements from the subject matter, some of which are facts, some opinion. Present them to students and have them determine which is which. **Assess** the students by giving them a new set of statements and have them identify which are facts and non-facts.

Subjective reasoning. Find examples of biased or subjective reasoning in a particular subject area. Start with easy examples such as from a television show for youth. Have students identify what interests the bias is trying to protect.

Identify objective reasoning. Present examples of objective and subjective reasoning and have students determine which is which.

Education or propaganda? According to Max Wertheimer (in Pratkanis & Aronson, 1992), propaganda "tries to keep people from thinking and from acting as humans with rights; it manipulates prejudice and emotion to impose the propagandist's will on others" (p. 266). Education provides people with the skills of self-reliance and democracy.

Fact or opinion? Have students read a newspaper or a magazine report or a story that presents actions and opinions. Have them make a list of what elements are facts and which are opinions.

Supporting opinion with the facts. Have students read arguments from two sides of an issue and take a position. Ask them to list which facts support their opinion and which do not.

Starred ✸ activities within each subskill go together!

Reasoning Generally
by Reasoning Objectively
Ideas for Developing Skills

Level 2: Attention to Facts and Skills
Focus on detail and prototypical knowledge, Build knowledge

What are facts in a particular subject area? Discuss how facts are based on empirical (observable, or research-based) evidence, and how they shouldn't mix in opinion or emotion. (1) Invite an expert from a particular discipline and ask them to discuss the facts they look for when solving discipline-specific problems. (2) Direct students to find examples of facts and non-facts in a particular subject area. Have students report the facts and non-facts in a particular subject area problem and assess their thoroughness and accuracy.

Distinguishing impulsive and deliberate reasoning. Present to students various scenarios of impulsive and deliberate reasoning in complex situations via written stories or videos. Discuss with the students the differences between impulsive and deliberate reasoning and decision making made by the characters. Assess with multiple-choice, true-false, or short answer tests of impulsive and deliberate reasoning skills.

Types of reasoning biases. Discuss with students the following kinds of biases to which people are susceptible:

(1) Exaggerating the advantages of an alternative that the person favors. For example, Mike wants to buy a bike. He finds one that he loves that's a 12-speed, has cool colors, and is more than he can afford. He also sees one that is a 10-speed, good quality, and within his price range. Mike rationalizes to himself that the 12-speed is the one he should have because it has 2 more speeds than the other one.

(2) Minimizing the drawbacks of an alternative that the person likes. Mike tells himself that he can borrow the extra money he needs for the bike he likes from his dad, who just lent him money last week for some new athletic shoes.

(3) Denying possible negative consequences of a given alternative. If Mike were thinking more rationally about this purchase, he would admit to himself that his dad will not probably lend him any more money until he pays him back for the shoes.

(4) Minimizing the advantages of an alternative that the person doesn't like. Mike doesn't think that the good quality of the other bike is very important. He'd rather be seen on a cool, flashy bike than on something boring (though dependable).

(5) Exaggerating the disadvantages of alternatives. Mike thinks that no one at school will like him if he has the 10-speed bike because it is not cool.

Present a reasoning situation to students (like the bike example above). Ask students to brainstorm examples of each bias that people might use in the example situation. **Assess** student's knowledge and identification of types of reasoning biases with multiple-choice, true-false, or short answer tests.

Starred activities within each subskill go together!

Reasoning Generally by Reasoning Objectively
Ideas for Developing Skills

Level 2 (continued)

Identify objective and subjective reasoning in the news. Have students find news reports that use objective or subjective reasoning. Discuss what clues help us discern objective from subjective reasoning.

Identify objective and subjective reasoning on the internet. Have students find examples of both kinds of reasoning on the internet. Discuss what is needed to change subjective to objective reasoning.

Getting the facts. There are different sources of facts for different domains in life. In a specific domain, discuss with students how facts are valid, which are sought, which are unimportant. Ask students to define a topic or area of research that they are interested in and have them list the *valid* and *relevant* facts in that area. **Assess** students' findings.

Starred activities within each subskill go together!

Level 3: Practice Procedures
Set goals, Plan steps of problem solving, Practice skills

Identification of biases in thinking. Have students practice identifying their own and others' biases in the decision-making process, including identification of alternatives, judging of alternatives, and final judgment of the best alternative. Use examples from periodicals of local disputes, from international disputes, from a particular classroom subject matter, or intercultural examples. Have students identify alternatives and reasons mentioned, identify possible underlying biases, and suggest an alternative supported by unbiased reason. **Assess** this process.

Getting the right facts for problem-solving. Have students identify the types of information that are factually important for a particular discipline. Then have students specify which facts they need (which questions to ask) in order to solve a particular problem in the discipline. They should then try to solve the problem with the help of an expert, or alone, with their success judged by an expert.

Level 4: Integrate Knowledge and Procedures
Execute plans, Solve problems

Reasoning objectively in particular subject matter. Have students prepare a report on a specific topic in a subject area. Ask them to use only objective reasoning. Ask an expert to evaluate how well they did.

Reasoning Generally by Using Sound Reasoning

Creative and Expert Implementer Real-Life Examples

Marie Curie was an expert in scientific reasoning. Through her scientific experiments, she discovered the radioactivity of certain elements. Her discoveries have made great contributions to science and are the basis not only for some of our energy sources today, but also for many current medical treatments (such as chemotherapy).

Ideas for Developing Skills

Level 1: Immersion in Examples and Opportunities
Attend to the big picture, Learn to recognize basic patterns

Is it true? Select one or two of the persuasive techniques listed in the chart. (1) Look at media (e.g., advertising in magazines, internet, television) to find examples of their usage. Then use Sagan's Baloney Detection suggestions to refute them. (2) Read a text and look for the persuasive techniques. Identify a better way to present the argument based on Sagan's suggestions. (3) Watch television for a half hour and mark down how many of these techniques are used. (4) Help students learn to talk back to the television when persuasive techniques are used to manipulate them.

Persuasive Techniques
- Use a vivid example or a testimonial.
- Use an authority figure's endorsement.
- Be vague about the specific numbers.
- Suggest that coincidences are causal relationships.
- Put two things together to make it seem like they are related.
- Refer to familiar things.
- Present something over and over so that it's the first thing that pops into a person's mind.

The Fine Art of Baloney Detection
(from Sagan, 1997, *The demon-haunted world: Science as a candle in the dark*)

What to do to evaluate the validity of a claim:
- Wherever possible there must be independent confirmation of the facts.
- Encourage substantive debate on the evidence by knowledgeable advocates of all points of view.
- Arguments from authorities carry little weight—they make mistakes. In science there are no authorities, just experts.
- Spin more than one hypothesis and think of the tests required to prove it.
- Try not to get overly attached to one hypothesis just because it's yours. Think of reasons to reject it. If you don't, others will.
- Quantify. If you can measure something, you are better able to discriminate among competing hypotheses. What is vague and qualitative is open to many explanations and truth is harder to find.
- If there is a chain of argument, **every** link in the chain must work (including the premise)—not just most of them.
- *Occam's razor.* When you have a choice, choose the simplest hypothesis.
- Always ask whether the hypothesis can be, at least in principle, falsified. Propositions that are untestable, unfalsifiable are not worth much.

Reasoning Generally
by Using Sound Reasoning
Ideas for Developing Skills

Level 1 (continued)

Defining sound reasoning. To determine if an argument or stated reasoning is sound, a person must determine two things. (1) Does the conclusion logically follow from the preceding statement? (2) Is the preceding statement (or premise) true? Discuss what this means so that students can learn basic patterns of sound reasoning. Give examples of unsound reasoning to students, some with weak logic and some with un-ture premises, and have students identify whether they are unsound and why. Use examples, such as:

- Preceding statement (or premise): Dark clouds are coming this way and the wind is picking up.
- Logical conclusion: A storm is approaching. Therefore, we should roll up the windows in the car.
- Illogical conclusion: It's going to be a nice day, so we should go swimming.
- Untrue preceding statement (or premise): The sun is purple (and so it is turning the clouds purple).

Level 2: Attention to Facts and Skills
Focus on detail and prototypical knowledge, Build knowledge

Arguments from authorities. Opinions of authorities should carry little weight on their own because individual authorities can make mistakes. Discuss examples from advertising in which a doctor advocates a particular product. Discuss why their endorsement might be a poor reason for selecting the product, even though it might be emotionally appealing.

Quantifying or using numbers to support your argument. Sometimes using measurements helps you discriminate among competing ideas or hypotheses. Vague statements without numbers are difficult to refute. (1) Discuss issues in a particular domain that generate disagreements. What measurements can be used to help determine which arguments are more plausible? (2) Identify common stereotypes and examine their validity based on statistics. For example, people think that African Americans commit more crime or use welfare more. A look at the statistics will contradict these impressions.

Identifying the elements of logic. Have students practice identifying the premises, conclusions, and logic indicators (e.g., since, thus, implies, consequently, because, so, if) in simple logic statements. Then have them evaluate whether the conclusion follows from the premise. Examples:

- We haven't seen a bird all day, so there must be no birds in this area.
- Tom will win the race this year because he won the race last year and has trained hard this year.
- If you don't go to other people's funerals, they won't go to yours.
- Cats can swim; thus my cat Barry can swim.

> "Critical thinking is the ability and willingness to assess claims and make objective judgments on the basis of well-supported reasons. It is the ability to look for flaws in arguments and resist claims that have no supporting evidence...It also fosters the ability to be creative and constructive—to generate possible explanations for findings, think of implications, and apply new knowledge to a broad range of social and personal problems."
>
> Carole Wade and Carol Tavris,
> *Creative and Critical Thinking* (pp. 4-5)

Starred activities within each subskill go together!

Reasoning Generally
by Using Sound Reasoning
Ideas for Developing Skills

Level 2 (continued)

Having adequate support for conclusions. In many situations, students must seek and obtain information themselves and then make a conclusion based on the information they have. An important skill they must learn (besides gathering accurate information, see EJ-1 for activities) is to obtain **enough** and the **right** kind of information to adequately support a conclusion. Choose an issue and have students state a possible conclusion for the issue. Then brainstorm as a class what kind of information would support the conclusion, what kind of information would contradict the conclusion, and how much support is needed for the conclusion to be strong.

Use critical thinking (from Wade & Tavris, 1993, *Critical and Creative Thinking*). Critical thinking is a process that involves the following: (1) ask questions; be willing to wonder; (2) define the problem; (3) examine the evidence; (4) analyze assumptions and biases; (5) avoid emotional reasoning; (6) don't oversimplify; (7) consider other interpretations; (8) tolerate uncertainty. Give the students one or two issues to which they can apply the critical thinking process. For example, why are some schools underachieving?

Level 3: Practice Procedures
Set goals, Plan steps of problem solving, Practice skills

Sound reasoning in scientific reasoning. (1) Describe to the students what scientific reasoning is (based on the scientific method), then have them apply it in a particular assignment or project. (2) Invite a scientist as a guest speaker to discuss the steps he or she takes to ensure impartial reasoning in his or her daily work. See the chart on the right.

Chains of argument. Important to reasoning well is the use of arguments. If there is a chain of arguments, every link in the chain must work (including the premise)—not just most of them. Present common issues in a particular domain (e.g., global warming, advertising to children, advertising tobacco or alcohol, use of the internet). Initially, present several hypotheses and the facts that support them. Point out the necessary elements in drawing a reasonable conclusion. In a later lesson, present reasoning about the issues that lacks a connecting argument or is incomplete (e.g., global warming isn't happening because this winter is the coldest in many years), and have students identify the places where reasoning breaks down. Have students apply what they learned in a new context by presenting new issues similar to the one already studied.

One type of sound reasoning is **scientific reasoning,** which uses principles such as these:

- Scientists should investigate questions that can be tested.

- Hypotheses should be tested with controlled studies.

- Theories should be based on empirical evidence.

- Generalizations should be made cautiously.

- All methods, theories, and conclusions should be reviewed by professional colleagues.

EJ-1 Reasoning Generally

Starred ★ activities within each subskill go together!

Reasoning Generally by Using Sound Reasoning
Ideas for Developing Skills

Reasons for rejecting an argument. When reasoning, it is important to not get overly attached to one hypothesis just because it is yours. Present hypotheses in a particular domain and ask students to think of reasons to reject it based on what they know. Then divide the reasons into good reasons and poor reasons (based on Sagan's criteria listed in this section). Do this regularly for topics being studied.

Occam's razor. An important general tool to use when trying to understand a phenomenon is *Occam's razor*—that when you have a choice, choose the simplest hypothesis. Present different issues and different hypotheses that people use to explain them. Based on what they know in the domain, ask students to identify which hypothesis is the simplest. For example, some people claim that alien abduction is the best explanation for the abduction experiences that people say they have had. A simpler reason, that has much more empirical evidence, is that the individuals were in a semi-dream state when the 'abductions' occurred.

Structured controversy. The steps for structured academic controversy (Johnson & Johnson, 1997), involving sound reasoning, are as follows:
(1) Select an issue relevant to what you are studying. Select two or more opinions on the issue.
(2) Form advocacy teams by putting the students into groups for each different opinion. Either put together a list of supporting statements for each opinion, or have students research the opinion and come up with their own supporting statements (if this is done, provide guidance and feedback for the accuracy and comprehensiveness of the supporting statements they generate). Each group prepares a persuasive statement based on the support-ing statements of their opinion.
(3) Have each group present its persuasive case to the other groups without interruption. Students in the listening groups should listen carefully and take notes to learn the other opinion well. Students listening should also evalu-ate the other positions based on the logic and soundness of the position.
(4) Have open discussion among the groups with advocacy of their own position and refutation of other positions (respectfully), specifically based on how sound their position or argument is.
(5) Groups trade positions on the issue to take another group's perspective. The group must present the other perspective to the others as sincerely and persuasively as the original group did. The group can add new facts, informa-tion, or arguments to the position (based on what they have already learned) to make it more persuasive.
(6) All individuals drop their advocacy and group-orientation to discuss the positions again and try to come to a consensus about which position has the soundest argument, looking at the logic of the argument and supporting evidence of the position. The position can be one that is a synthesis of two or more, as long as the position's argument is deemed to be sound by all individuals and isn't just a compromise.

Starred ★ activities within each subskill go together!

Reasoning Generally
by Using Sound Reasoning
Ideas for Developing Skills

Level 3 (continued)

Making an argument on a social issue. Have each student choose a debated social issue (e.g., animal rights, nuclear power) and take a stance on the issue. (1) Have students put together a set of arguments to support their viewpoint. Emphasize to students that the goal of the exercise is to have enough supporting evidence to make a strong conclusion. Break this exercise into steps: (a) choosing an appropriate issue, (b) finding information and evidence about their issue, (c) determining how much evidence is needed for a strong conclusion, and (e) writing an essay containing a description of the issue, the supporting evidence, and the conclusion. (2) Have students find all the arguments against their position. Then have them respond to the arguments with the evidence they collected previously. **Assess** the student's essay for each of the points named above.

Evaluating arguments in debates and constructing their own argument. Either set up a student debate on a particular issue or have students watch a debate. Before the debate, discuss the issue with the class and have them jot down arguments they think are particularly strong in the issue and why. After the debate, have the class write down what the strong arguments were that were made by the debate participants. Have them compare and contrast them to the ideas they jotted down before the argument.

Be open-minded. Part of critical thinking is the ability to stand back from your own perspective and look at things from another perspective. Have students practice doing this with a list of creative statements. For example: Statement 1: "The best time to eat an orange is at 5 pm." Open-minded response: "Well, perhaps there is research that shows that the vitamins of an orange are best absorbed at 5 pm." Statement 2: "Baseball is the best sport." Open-minded response: "Well, it's true that it has a long history in the United States and people of all ages play it, or play softball which is similar."

Be skeptical. Part of critical thinking is the ability to criticize your own perspective and others that are presented to you. Have students practice doing this by first generating a list of things they believe. Then have them critically dialogue back and forth with each statement. To avoid sensitive issues, the teacher can collect the lists and then select a few from the whole class for the whole class to work on. For example, Belief 1: "I believe that eating chocolate is good for me." Criticism: "How do you know that? Are you sure that you are not just saying that because it tastes good?" Response: "Research shows that dark chocolate has stearic acid which is good for you." Criticism: "Where did you hear that? Are you sure it is a credible source?" Response: "I read it in a science magazine."

Starred ★ activities within each subskill go together!

Reasoning Generally
by Using *Sound* Reasoning
Ideas for Developing Skills

Level 4: Integrate Knowledge and Procedures
Execute plans, Solve problems

Mentoring others in decision-making. Assign students a younger student who needs assistance in an area of reasoning. Prepare the older students carefully so they can model sound reasoning. (Lack of preparation may leave both students frustrated.)

Proving it. When you have a hypothesis, make sure to prepare for the possibility that it is wrong. One way to do this is to generate more than one hypothesis to think of the tests required to prove them. (1) Present issues to students, and ask them to generate hypotheses and tests for each hypothesis. (2) Have them test one or more of the hypotheses with the tests they designed.

★ **Setting up and implementing debates.** Have students design and implement their own debate on a relevant topic. **Assess** students by having them write an essay, taking a stance on the issue and constructing their own argument by using sound and supportive information.

Justify your viewpoint. According to Gutmann and Thompson (*Democracy and Disagreement*, 1996, p. 65), critical thinking is fundamental to developing one's capacities as a democratic citizen. It requires the ability to justify one's actions, to criticize the actions of fellow citizens and to respond to their corresponding justifications and criticisms. Have students practice justifying actions in one or more of the following ways: (1) In a story or history lesson, have them take a position within a disagreement and justify it. Make sure to discuss the difference between good and poor justifications. (2) Students investigate a social issue about which they do not have an opinion. Have them justify the positions of opposing sides. (3) Have the students create two versions of an ad for a product, one using good justifications and one using poor justifications. Present them to the class and have the class analyze the quality of justifications used.

Assessment Hints

Using sound reasoning

Use multiple-choice, true-false, short answer, or essay tests to assess student's knowledge of sound reasoning skills.

Present new examples of unsound reasoning to students, some with weak logic and some with untrue premises, and have students identify whether they are unsound and why.

Give logic statements/problems to students and have them identify the premises, conclusions, and logic indicators.

Present an argument and have the students evaluate its strength (i.e., how much information is presented to support the issue and how well the information supports the issue).

Starred ★ activities within each subskill go together!

Reasoning Generally
by Avoiding Reasoning Pitfalls

Creative and Expert Implementer Real-Life Example

Medical researchers have to be very careful to avoid human reasoning pitfalls, such as observational selection (explained on p. 59). If they are not careful, their research and work could mean death for some patients.

Ideas for Developing Skills

Level 1: Immersion in Examples and Opportunities
Attend to the big picture, Learn to recognize basic patterns

Reasoning fallacies. Select one or more of Sagan's (1997) "Fallacies of Logic and Rhetoric" (p. 59). Present examples of the fallacy, and ask students to figure out the flaw. After students are familiar with the type of fallacy, ask them to find or create more examples. For example: (1) <u>Ad hominem:</u> Use statements from someone but attack the person not the statement (e.g., John says that 2 plus 2 is 4 but he's ugly so what does he know?) (2) <u>Observational selection</u> (confirmatory bias): Present a video of a character and secretly tell half the class that the person is stupid and they should look for all the stupid things he or she does; tell the other half of the class (also secretly) that the person is smart and they should look for all the smart things he or she did. Afterwards, ask groups to write down the stupid things and the smart things. Ask them to compare their lists, showing that people often see what they are looking for. The list of what was looked for should be much longer.

Level 2: Attention to Facts and Skills
Focus on detail and prototypical knowledge, Build knowledge

Weasel words. People often use acceptable words to label their less than acceptable goals or ideas (e.g., Inter-Continental Ballistic Missile [ICBM] = peacekeeper; collateral damage for civilians killed in military action). Have students look for or generate a list of terms that each mask the true meaning of the real idea they express.

Statistics of small numbers, or generalizing from a few cases. For a particular domain, give students sets of statements, some of which are based on anecdotal evidence (a couple of cases) and others that are based on large numbers. Discuss how a vivid example can draw our attention and make us forget the numbers that contradict the example. For example: "The Surgeon General says that smoking tobacco greatly increases a person's chances of dying young (or getting some disease). But my uncle smoked and he lived till he was 99."

Don't be snowed. Have students find examples of advertisements or salesmen that use a snow job (i.e., they overwhelm you with misleading information).

Sort fact from bunk. Have students find examples of advertisements that use facts and those that use white lies or make you infer a mistaken conclusion.

Starred ★ activities within each subskill go together!

Reasoning Generally
by Avoiding Reasoning Pitfalls
Ideas for Developing Skills

Starred ★ activities
within each subskill
go together!

Level 2 (continued)

Suppressed evidence, or half-truths. Present examples of half-truths from a particular domain and have students find more examples. Point out in the examples why the statements are half-truths. Have students think of what evidence is needed to make the half-truths into "full" truths. For example, "Toothpaste X is the toothpaste most recommended by dentists [based on 3% of the dentists who responded to our survey sent to 1,000 dentists around the country]." The added information in brackets is not given to the viewers so it sounds like most dentists really like toothpaste X, when in reality, only 3% of the sampled dentists responded, and out of those 30, most but not all of them still did not choose X.

Straw man, or caricaturing a position – misrepresenting it – to make it easier to attack. In arguing for his/her own position on an issue, the person may resort to misrepresenting the other position to make it easier to attack. Find an example in a news show in which two people on different sides of an issue misrepresent the other side. Use the issue as a class research project, in which the students research the issue and find the facts, opinions, and arguments of each side of the issue. Then present the news show and have students discuss how one side (or both) misrepresented the other side. Note: this activity can also be done with academic journal articles instead of news shows.

Assessment Hints

Avoiding human reasoning pitfalls

Use multiple-choice, true-false, short answer, or essay tests to assess student's knowledge of reasoning pitfalls.

Present new examples of reasoning pitfalls to students and have students identify what they are.

Have students find examples of reasoning pitfalls in a particular subject area and assess their examples.

Level 3: Practice Procedures
Set goals, Plan steps of problem solving, Practice skills

★ **Confusion of correlation and causation**. Discuss how confusing correlation and causation can lead to erroneous reasoning. Have students find or create examples. An example of confusing correlation and causation would be "I, as a teenager, am sleepy in the morning. This may be because the sun rises in the morning." – *Not*. Research shows that teens both need more sleep and are on a delayed sleeping shift—finding it hard to get to sleep before midnight.

Non sequitur, or linking unrelated claims. Have students find or create examples, such as, "Our nation will prevail because God is great" and "you're short so I'm smarter."

Post hoc, ergo propter hoc, or it happened after X so it was caused by X. Find examples of this kind of reasoning or have students make them up. For example, the Vikings won after I stopped going to their games, so they won because I didn't go. **Assess** by putting together a set of problematic statements (based on the Sagan list of fallacies) and have the students indicate what is wrong (what fallacy is evident) in each statement.

Reasoning Generally
by Avoiding Reasoning Pitfalls
Ideas for Developing Skills

Level 3 (continued)

Inconsistency in a subject area. It is inconsistent to say that the decline of life expectancy in the former Soviet Union is due to failure of communism without a comparable statement that the high infant mortality rate in the U.S. is due to the failure of capitalism. Find examples of this kind of reasoning or have students make them up, relevant to the subject area. **Assess** by putting together a set of problematic statements (based on the Sagan list of fallacies) and have the students indicate what fallacy is evident in each statement.

Starred ★ activities within each subskill go together!

Level 4: Integrate Knowledge and Procedures
Execute plans, Solve problems

Creating, exchanging, and correcting reasoning pitfalls. Have groups of students write about an issue, intentionally adding multiple reasoning pitfalls into the paper. The groups exchange papers and identify which reasoning pitfalls were used in the paper and how they should be corrected.

What not to do: Fallacies of Logic and Rhetoric

- *ad hominem* (Latin: "to the man")—attacking the arguer (the person) and not the argument
- argument from authority ('So-and-so says..')
- argument from the adverse consequences that will result if hypothesis rejected
- appeal to ignorance—the claim that whatever has not been proved false must be true, and vice versa. Absence of evidence is not evidence of absence.
- special pleading, often to rescue a proposition in deep rhetorical trouble (e.g., "God moves in mysterious ways")
- begging the question (assuming the answer)
- observational selection (confirmatory belief)—counting the hits and ignoring the misses (noticing only the evidence that supports your claim and ignoring all the rest)
- statistics of small numbers (generalizing from a few cases)
- misunderstanding of the nature of statistics
- inconsistency (e.g., to say that the decline of life expectancy in the former Soviet Union is due to failure of communism without a comparable statement that the high infant mortality rate in the U.S. is due to the failure of capitalism)
- *non sequitur* (linking unrelated claims, e.g., "Our nation will prevail because God is great")
- *post hoc, ergo propter hoc* (Latin: it happened after X so it was caused by X)
- excluded middle ground or false dichotomy (it's either one extreme position or the other)
- slippery slope, related to excluded middle (there is no middle ground)
- confusion of correlation and causation (In summer ice cream sales and rapes increase—this doesn't mean that eating ice cream causes rapes. It has to do with a third variable—warm weather.)
- straw man—caricaturing a position (misrepresenting it) to make it easier to attack
- suppressed evidence/ half-truths
- weasel words (InterContinental Ballistic Missile [ICBM] = "peacekeeper")

Create a Climate
to Develop General Reasoning

- Encourage students' commitment to use reason to make decisions. Discuss with them human tendencies to lose control (and do harm) when emotions are high.

- Encourage students to carefully and systematically think about a problem.

- Acknowledge that many decisions are made with intuition but that intuition is trained by experience (like culture) and can produce biases against new people and ideas. Working on reasoning skills helps you intervene when your instinctive intuitions are based on harmful bias.

- Have the student refer to his or her value commitments regularly for completing assignments.

- Promote students' feeling and taking responsibility/accountability for one's own actions. Discipline students with immediate consequences and a given reason. Help parents with discipline plans that include giving reasons to students when disciplined. Discuss related dilemmas with slight variations.

- Encourage students' commitment to be impartial when they have time to reason throughout the judgment process. Discuss human tendencies to favor one individual over another, or not consider all options, or to misjudge the probability of consequences occurring.

Sample Student Self-Monitoring
Developing General Reasoning Skills
Encourage active learning by having students learn to monitor their own learning

Reasoning objectively
Am I thinking carefully about the problem and my reasons?
Am I distinguishing facts from non-facts?
Am I exaggerating the advantages of an alternative I favor?
Am I minimizing the drawbacks of an alternative that I favor?
Am I minimizing the advantages of an alternative that I don't like?
Am I not considering the possible negative consequences of an alternative I favor?
Am I exaggerating the disadvantages of an alternative that I don't like?

Using sound reasoning
Am I thinking logically about my reasons?
Do I have enough support for the conclusions or decisions I am making?
Does the information that I am basing my reasoning on have independent confirmation of the facts?
Have I considered all of the evidence by knowledgeable advocates on all points of view?
Have I thought of more than one hypothesis to explain the issue?
Am I overly attached to one particular hypothesis?
Have I quantified what I am measuring?
Does EVERY link in my chain of argument work?
Have I chosen the simplest hypothesis?
Can my hypothesis be falsified?

Avoiding human reasoning pitfalls
Am I attacking the argument or the person making the argument?
Am I blindly accepting the argument from an authority?
Am I making an unwarranted special pleading that provides no empirical support?
Am I taking into account ALL of the evidence (and not selectively ignoring the evidence that does not support my position)?
Am I generalizing from a few cases and ignoring the large numbers?
Am I being inconsistent in making comparative arguments?
Are the claims that I am making unrelated?
Are the causal claims I am making logical and plausible?
Could the causal claim I am making have a third variable that I am not considering?
Is there a middle-ground argument or position that I am not considering?
Am I accurately representing the position I am arguing against?
Is any of my evidence half-truths?
Are any of my words or terms misleading?

Selections to Post in the Classroom
for Reasoning Generally

DISPOSITIONS OF CRITICAL THINKING
(Ennis, 1987)

- Seek a clear statement of the thesis or question
- Seek reasons
- Be well informed
- Use and mention credible sources
- Consider the total situation
- Keep to the main point
- Keep in mind the original or basic concern
- Look for alternatives
- Be open-minded
- Take a position when the evidence and reasons are sufficient to support that position
- Seek as much precision as the subject permits
- Deal in an orderly manner with the parts of a complex whole
- Use critical thinking abilities (skills)
- Be sensitive to others' feelings, level of knowledge, and degree of sophistication
- Use one's critical thinking abilities

Reasoning Ethically
(Decide right and wrong)

WHAT
Students make judgments and decisions every day about how to get along with others. Students use ethical reasoning to make each and every one of these decisions. In using ethical reasoning, they think about what codes, rules, laws, or ideals a person should be following, which is the most fair, just, kind, dutiful action and what outcomes a decision may bring about.

WHY
Just as general reasoning skills are necessary to function and participate in today's complex society, so are ethical reasoning skills. More highly developed forms of ethical reasoning are positively related to a number of constructs and behaviors, including but not limited to

- ethical behavior (Thoma, 1994)
- decision making and job performance in specific professions (Rest & Narvaez, 1994)
- a concern for others and a stronger sense of lessons learned in past experiences (Pratt, Norris, Arnold, & Filyer, 1999)
- leadership status and number of close friendships (Schonert-Reichl, 1999)
- strength of conscience in adolescence (Hart, 1988)

SUBSKILLS OVERVIEW
Judging perspectives
Reasoning about standards and ideals
Reasoning about actions and outcomes

Contexts
for Ethical Decision Making

For media literacy	At school
With friends	On the street
In public places	In businesses

EJ-2 Reasoning Ethically

Web Wise
The Peace Corps' World Wise Schools had resources and ideas for global education:
    www.peacecorps.gov/wws
http://www.instituteonraceandpoverty.org
Center for Diversity Education: http://www.diversityed.org

Ideas for Promoting Ethical Judgment in the Classroom

Students develop their judgments about getting along with others in the following sequence. In order to stimulate growth, teachers can design the classroom in many different ways. Teachers' behavior in the classroom fosters particular types of reasoning:

Personal Interest Reasoning
- Teachers should focus on discipline/setting limits.
- Teachers should encourage children to learn cooperative skills by using cooperative learning, peer mediation, and conflict resolution.
- Teachers should use role playing, simulations, and discussion to encourage good peer relations and avoid discrimination against differences.

Maintaining Norms Reasoning
- Teachers should set up bilateral agreements with student groups to meet current needs.

Post-Conventional Reasoning
- Teachers should emphasize choosing behavior that would be expected of others in similar circumstances and foster discussions about how an ideal society should be established.

Reasoning Ethically by Judging Perspectives

The chief prosecutor for war crimes in the former Yugoslavia **Carla del Ponte** is famous for her ruthless pursuit of organized crime. When Ms. Del Ponte took up her new role with the UN on 15 September 1999, bringing the former Serb leader to justice became her top priority. But her mission did not end with his imprisonment. She has sworn not to rest until all the major players responsible for the atrocities in the Balkans have been brought to justice.

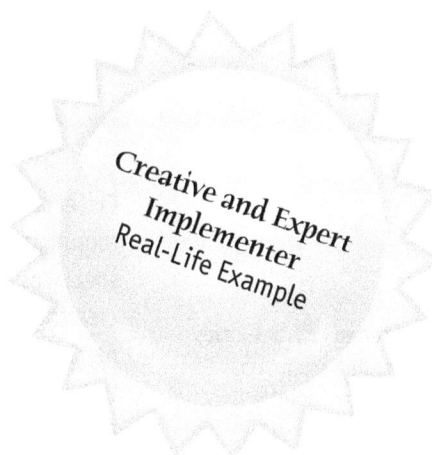

Creative and Expert Implementer Real-Life Example

Ideas for Developing Skills

Level 1: Immersion in Examples and Opportunities
Attend to the big picture, Learn to recognize basic patterns

A look at perspectives in reasoning biases. (1) <u>Fiction</u>. Use a film or story that presents the story differently depending on the character who is telling the story (e.g., Japanese film *Rashamon*, story *Moonstone*) (2) <u>Real simulation</u>. Watch the film *Brown Eyes, Blue Eyes* or read the book about it. Discuss how one's circumstances can change one's perspective.

Perspectives on a controversial case. Have students gather information about reactions to a controversial case (e.g., the OJ Simpson trial, Rodney King police officer trial). Discuss the different perspectives on guilt and innocence and what might have caused the difference in perspectives.

Television judge. Bring in an excerpt from a court television how that gives the two perspectives and how the judge judges the perspectives. Before the judge gives a verdict, have students discuss what they think the verdict should be.

Level 2: Attention to Facts and Skills
Focus on detail and prototypical knowledge, Build knowledge

Impartiality in the legal system. Bring in a local judge to discuss the nature of impartiality. Focus on the relationship between impartiality and fairness. How does impartiality help the judge make fair decisions? How does the judge practice impartiality?

Stepping outside the box. Give students an ethical dilemma of in-group versus out-group. Students practice taking the perspective of the out-group members (i.e. stepping outside the box) and make their decision using that perspective. For example, out-group members could be people who live in another country, another city, in another culture or religion, who are extremely poor, who are ill, who are elderly. Have students discuss why it is important to take the perspective of out-group members.

Starred ★ activities within each subskill go together!

Reasoning Ethically
by Judging Perspectives
Ideas for Developing Skills

Starred ★ activities within each subskill go together!

Level 2 (continued)

Criteria for judging perspectives in a subject area. Discuss agreed-upon criteria for judging the validity of a perspective in a particular subject area. For example, perspectives on biodiversity can be examined from a scientific perspective (are humans creating conditions to eliminate plant and animal life at a record rate?), a historical perspective (is the world progressing or regressing?), and a social studies perspective (is industrial development of a nation better than not?). Distinguish using the agreed-upon criteria from using pure feeling. Show examples from the subject area. After some aided practice, have students work in groups on specific problems, applying the criteria.

Level 3: Practice Procedures
Set goals, Plan steps of problem solving, Practice skills

★ **Bias in judgments.** Discuss the following facts (or others like them) and discuss what might be causing them:
- Women criminals tend to receive harsher punishments than men with the same records.
- African-American males tend to receive harsher punishments than white men with the same records.
- Tall men are more likely to get promoted, get the job, win the election.
- Fat women are more likely to not get promoted, not get the job, not win the election.

Have the students describe how they would practice impartiality to counter each of these facts (this can build on the Level 2 activity of impartiality).

Applying discipline for misbehavior. Discuss cases of peer misbehavior and how to make a decision about consequences. Use real or imaginary cases. Try to use a standard of impartiality. Discuss potential biases.

Public policy. Identify several public policy issues (e.g., freedom of speech for hate groups, right to carry handguns, abortion, etc.) or policy issues in your own community. Have students identify the positions that people have on the issue and what perspective that different individuals bring to the issues that affects their judgment. Let students select criteria for juding the validity of the positions and apply them. Students report on their work.

Level 4: Integrate Knowledge and Procedures
Execute plans, Solve problems

★ **Courtroom role play.** Select an issue of interest to the students. Set up a role play with judge, lawyers, jury, and accused. Have jury or rest of class keep track of perspectives and make a final judgment.

Assessment Hints

Judging perspectives

Use multiple-choice, true-false, short answer, or essay tests to assess students' knowledge of judging perspectives and detecting bias in others' perspectives.

Present new examples of biased and unbiased reasoning to students and have students identify whether they are biased and why.

Reasoning Ethically
by Reasoning about Standards and Ideals

One of the most influential moral philosophers in history, **Immanuel Kant** was an expert in reasoning about standards and ideals. Kant argued that moral principles are categorical imperatives, or absolute standards of reason that have no exceptions and cannot be related to pleasure or practical benefit. Kant said that telling a lie is wrong.

Creative and Expert Implementer Real-Life Example

Ideas for Developing Skills

Level 1: Immersion in Examples and Opportunities
Attend to the big picture, Learn to recognize basic patterns

Judging codes. (1) Students conduct research on how groups or individuals (e.g., religious leaders, city councils, state legislators, bioethicists) decide which codes are valid and which invalid (e.g., religious tradition, community tradition, reason, expert wisdom). (2) Interview an elder about a specific set of codes. How does the elder decide whether or not the code is a good one? (3) Sometimes codes can only be judged when they are applied because they can be applied in different ways. Find examples of this in a particular domain or culture.

Stories and essays addressing ideals. Students read texts that focus on an ideal (e.g., justice: *Les Miserables,* benevolence: *The Giving Tree,* beauty: *Strong Wind*, truth: *King Solomon and the two mothers*). Students identify the definition of the ideal in the text and explain how it applies in the story and how it might apply in their lives.

Exploring reasoning in other judgment processes. Explore with the students the different kinds of judgment processes used in your own and different communities (e.g. U.S. legal system, peace circles, community mediation). If possible, invite an individual who works in one of these judgment processes. Discuss with students how reasoning about standards and ideals is a judgment process.

Community members' experiences of ideals and standards. Have students interview non-relative adult community members about one of the following ideals: justice, truth, benevolence, or beauty. Students ask the community member to tell them a story about an experience of justice, truth, benevolence, or beauty, in which she or he better understood the ideal by seeing or experiencing how it was upheld or violated. Have students present their interview findings to the class.

⭐

Starred ⭐ activities within each subskill go together!

Reasoning Ethically by Reasoning about Standards and Ideals
Ideas for Developing Skills

Level 2: Attention to Facts and Skills
Focus on detail and prototypical knowledge, Build knowledge

Creating reasons for options. In decision-making situations, a person thinks of all possible options, and then chooses one of those options based on a reason. Present an ethical dilemma to the students. Have students practice generating reasons for as many options as possible, focusing on reasons that are based on standards and ideals. In small groups, have the students generate reasons, based on standards and ideals, for as many options as possible. **Assess** students by having them complete this activity individually.

Domain standards. Invite an expert from a particular field of study to class. Ask the expert to identify the standards of excellence in their area of work, why the standards are important (socially), how the standards are instituted in their field, and how this affects the expert's work in the field. For example, a health professional could talk about standard of care and equal distribution of care; a judge could talk about the standard of justice and how this is ensured in the legal system.

My standards and ideals. Students identify the standards and ideals of their heritage with one of the following activities, then write an essay about what they learn. Questions they explore during the activity should include: What are the sources for the standards and ideals? How are the sources accessed? How does one respect the standards and ideals? What happens when one violates them? (1) Students interview parents or guardians about the standards and ideals they hold in the family. (2) Students interview community elders (religious or cultural) about the standards and ideals of the community. (3) Students find information on the internet or in the library.

Exploring standards in a subject area. Have students obtain information about the standards for excellence in a particular subject area (e.g., scientific research, legal system, business). Discuss how these standards compare and contrast with standards in other areas of study.

Violation of ideals. After exploring what the ideals mean according to scholars and community members, bring it to a personal level. Students discuss what instances of justice and injustice can look like. Have students discuss (or journal) personal experiences of injustice. Do the same for experiences of lack of truth, benevolence, or beauty.

Starred activities within each subskill go together!

Reasoning Ethically by Reasoning about Standards and Ideals
Ideas for Developing Skills

Level 2 (continued)

Forms of duty: Obligations and commitments. Have students find out about an adult family member's obligations and commitments. Contrast these with their own obligations and commitments. Define and contrast the standards each uses and then have the students describe and discuss how commitments and obligations influence the ethical decision-making process. Use a specific issue that interests them: for example, wanting to be with friends when one has an obligation.

Understanding benevolence. Define and contrast different forms of benevolence with the students (e.g., kindness, charity, altruism, self-sacrifice). (1) Students discuss how they have seen these ideals implemented in their own community and what effects they had. (2) Students think about how they have shown these concepts in their own past behaviors, or how they can show them in future behavior. (3) Students describe and discuss how these concepts influence the ethical decision-making process in general and in particular situations (e.g., discuss a dilemma).

Ethical dilemmas in a particular field. Identify a real-life ethical dilemma in a particular field and an expert who would be willing to come to class to discuss ideals of the field and their relation to the ethical dilemma. **Assess** by having students write an essay about the dilemma afterwards and have the expert assess them.

Level 3: Practice Procedures
Set goals, Plan steps of problem solving, Practice skills

Personal balance sheet with standards (based on Mann, Harmoni, & Power, 1991). Presented with an ethical dilemma, (a) students make a personal balance sheet, in which they have 2 columns with the headings of options and standards. Students list all options they can think of with their corresponding standards. (b) Students discuss with their parents/guardian. (c) Based on this discussion, students make a decision and state their reasoning (which should be based on community or family standards and ideals). (d) Students defend their positions in a group or classroom discussion.

Ethical dilemma discussions. Use hypothetical or classroom-based ethical dilemmas to start a discussion on what standards or ideals one can apply to making a decision about the dilemma. Make sure students are applying their religious/cultural/community codes. See Appendix for description of an ethical dilemma discussion. **Assess** by giving students a description of an ethical dilemma, and ask students to list all ethical actions that one could take to resolve the dilemma and to describe reasons (based on standards and ideals) for taking each action.

Starred ⭐ activities within each subskill go together!

EJ-2 Reasoning Ethically

Reasoning Ethically by Reasoning about Standards and Ideals
Ideas for Developing Skills

Reasoning about standards and ideals

Use multiple-choice, true-false, short answer, or essay tests to assess students' understanding of justice.

Present new ethical dilemmas to students and have students list the possible optional actions and reasons, based on standards and ideals, for each action.

Present different dilemmas based on different standards (e.g., justice, benevolence, obligations, etc.) and have students identify what standards apply to each dilemma.

Level 3 (continued)

Justice or ideals in ethical dilemmas. Present to the students ethical dilemmas that involve issues of justice that could happen (or have happened) in their community. Students explore what justice means in their community and apply it to the dilemmas. The students then discuss how concepts of justice can be applied in their reasoning and decision-making process. This activity can also be done with other standards such as benevolence and truth.

★ **Understanding ethical dilemmas in other cultures**. Discuss with students how ethical ideals may vary in other cultures. If appropriate, use cultural differences that exist in your community. For example, how would having one of the following ideals as a priority affect your deliberation about an ethical dilemma: (1) Obeying your elders; (2) Trying not to do anything wrong in this life that you will pay for in your next life; (3) Respecting creation. Ask students to apply their own religious/cultural perspectives.

Level 4: Integrate Knowledge and Procedures
Execute plans, Solve problems

Recognizing the ambiguity in ethical dilemmas and arguments. "Ethical dilemma" means that there is a clash of 2 or more values so that it is hard to decide on what is the best (most ethical) action to take. Present to the students real-life ethical dilemmas where there are no clear right or wrong answers. Facilitate a discussion with the students in which students identify the cultural/religious perspectives of the community in their discussion, including their own heritage.

★ **Ethical dilemmas involving multiple cultural differences**. Discuss the possible ideals behind ethical/moral practices in other cultures. If possible, use ethical/moral practices of different cultural groups within the community. Some concrete examples include girls not being able to wear the 'veil' in French classrooms, girls and women not being allowed in public without a male relative in Saudi Arabia, and boys being expected to sacrifice themselves for the Palestinian cause. Then have the students research the reasons behind the practice and the reasons given by those against the practice, using media resources and cultural experts. **Assess** the students' reports of their research results.

Starred ★ activities within each subskill go together!

Reasoning Ethically
by Reasoning about Actions & Outcomes

Supreme court justice, **Thurgood Marshall**, was an expert in reasoning about outcomes. He had a profound sense of social justice and made many decisions (some of them controversial) based on his deep commitment to justice and civil rights. During a time when racial segregation was the norm, Justice Marshall won the *Brown v. Board of Education* case. As Supreme Court Justice, Marshall opposed court decisions that supported arbitrary police practices, neglected the poor, or chipped away at civil rights. He was known for his principled judgments, which were not always popular in their time.

Creative and Expert Implementer Real-Life Example

Ideas for Developing Skills

Level 1: Immersion in Examples and Opportunities
Attend to the big picture, Learn to recognize basic patterns

Outcomes of legal cases in the news. Students bring in news stories about judgments that were made concerning transgressions of individuals. Discuss (a) what perspective the individual judged might have about the outcome and why (such as personal gain or loss), (b) what perspective the judge might have about the transgression and why (such as level of harm to the community), (c) public reaction to the case and what drives the reaction and (d) the perspective of the students' heritages (religious, cultural).

What is fair? Have students react to community- or school-related controversial issues with the following questions: What is there to be worried about? Who benefits or doesn't from the situation? What is a fair outcome and why? They should apply reasoning that includes their own religious/cultural codes to the discussion. Issues could include: (a) Hockey coach allowing his team to watch pornographic films in the hotel during away games. (b) Student cheating in order to get an A in a class. (c) Player cheating on the football field, pretending he caught a pass when it actually hit the ground.

Social justice. Students read about leaders for social justice and discuss why justice is important to these leaders. Have students find out about social justice in their own community, and find out which groups advocate for what kind of justice. Students report on what outcomes these groups would like to see as a result of their work in social justice. If looking at multiple kinds of social justice groups, students can compare the desired outcomes of the different groups.

Examples of reasoning about actions. Use examples from stories or films to show reasoning about what action to take. Films that have scenes where a character does this (e.g., *John Q* —early in the movie when John is trying to get money, *Little Women*).

Starred ★ activiti[es] within each subski[ll] go together!

EJ-2 Reasoning Ethically

Reasoning Ethically by Reasoning about Actions & Outcomes
Ideas for Developing Skills

Level 2: Attention to Facts and Skills
Focus on prototypical knowledge, Build knowledge

What is a good outcome? Select a particular ethical idea (justice, benevolence, truth, etc.) in a specific domain (parent's work, particular community issue, particular school issue). Have students investigate the nature of a good outcome based on using one of these ideals. How do people measure outcomes? What time line do they use? What is good? Have them interview elders and parents about their opinions. (NOTE: This activity can be paired with the starred activity in Reasoning about standards and ideals: Level 2. The community member could talk about what a good outcome was [or would/should have been] in his or her experience.

Thinking about fairness in ethical dilemmas. Present to the students ethical dilemmas that were solved one way or another. The dilemmas can be real-life dilemmas that occurred in school, the community, or the news; or dilemmas that appear in curricula content. The students then discuss the actual outcomes. What criteria did people apply in making a decision? How was the outcome positive or negative? **Assess** with essays on a teacher-selected or student-selected dilemma.

Thinking about preserving ideals in solving ethical dilemmas. Present to the students ethical dilemmas that involve issues of duty, loyalty, justice, benevolence, or another ideal. Use either (a) real-life dilemmas that occurred in school, the community or the news or (b) dilemmas that appear in curricula content. Students discuss how the ideal and be preserved in making a decision and what an outcome that preserves the ideal looks like.

Practice deciding about actions. When people decide about what action to take, they should ask themselves: (1) What moral rights does each person in the situation have and which action best respects and supports those rights? (2) What moral responsibilities do I have and what action best supports meeting my responsibilities? Have students answer these two questions when trying to resolve a dilemma or scenario. For example, (a) your friend wants you to go to a party but you have promised to visit your grandmother. (b) You see your friend steal a toy when you are with him/her in the store. (c) You have a choice to buy a CD from a local store or from a national chain store. (d) Your teammate asks you to cheat when you get the ball next during a competitive game with another school.

Starred ★ activities within each subskill go together!

What Students Need to Know to Seek Assistance in Making Ethical Judgments

- Where to seek help in deciding
- Who to ask for help
- How to ask for help
- How to use others' insight

Reasoning Ethically by Reasoning about Actions & Outcomes
Ideas for Developing Skills

Level 3: Practice Procedures
Set goals, Plan steps of problem solving, Practice skills

Focusing on outcomes in a particular domain. In order to make good decisions, people need a lot of information about the possible consequences of particular decisions. Within a particular domain, some outcomes are perceived to be better than others regardless of the side effects. In making a decision, people often emphasize some aspects of a problem more than others and minimize negative side effects. For example, in business, increasing sales and income is a priority for shareholders. If this requires laying off many people—a negative effect on employees—so be it because it is less important than the priority. Have students investigate (through interviews of people in the field, internet research, books, etc.) the desired outcomes in a particular domain (e.g., in medicine, it can be discovering a cure for a dreaded disease). Students should find out as much as they can about the side effects of positive outcomes. Report to class. If possible, have a local expert from a specific domain come to class and talk to students at some point during their investigation.

Personal balance sheet with outcomes (based on Mann, Harmoni, & Power, 1991). Present students with an ethical dilemma involving fairness or another ethical standard and have them make a personal balance sheet, in which they have 3 columns with the headings of options, codes, and outcomes. Students then list all options they can think of with their corresponding codes and possible outcomes in the next 2 columns. Students discuss the options and outcomes with their parents/guardian. Based on this information, students make a decision they think is most fair and state their reason behind it. They then defend it in a group or classroom discussion.

Ethical dilemma discussions. Use hypothetical or classroom-based ethical dilemmas to discuss what standards or ideals one can apply to making a decision about the dilemma AND what the outcomes would be for these applied ideals. Make sure students are applying their religious/cultural/community codes. See Appendix for description of an ethical dilemma discussion. Assess by giving students a description of an ethical dilemma. Ask them to describe all ethical actions one could take to resolve the dilemma and describe reasons (based on standards and ideals) for taking each action.

Prisoner's Dilemma. Present the students with a hypothetical case, which consists of 2 prisoners who go before a judge. In a plea-bargaining arrangement, the judge presents them with the possible options and consequences: (1) if only one confesses, the confessor will be released and the nonconfessor will go to jail for 10 years, (2) if both confess, both go to prison for 5 years, and (3) if neither confesses, both go to prison for a year. The students can then discuss what codes may be underlying each option and what the most ethical option would be. For specific details, see Kidder's (1995) *How Good People Make Tough Choices*, pp. 181-182.

Starred ★ activities within each subskill go together!

Reasoning Ethically by Reasoning about Actions & Outcomes
Ideas for Developing Skills

Level 3 (continued)

More issues in deciding about actions. There are many issues to think about when making a decision. Here are more questions to think about. (1) What positives and what negatives might each action create? (2) Which action will lead to the best overall outcome? (3) What action treats everyone the same (unless there is a moral reason not to) and does not favor or discriminate against anyone? (4) Which action enhances the well-being of the community? (5) Which action supports morality in others? Use the examples from Level 2 "Practice deciding about actions."

Level 4: Integrate Knowledge and Procedures
Execute plans, Solve problems

Ethical outcomes in a particular field. Have students work in a particular domain, identify problems and their resolutions, and determine if the outcomes were good for that domain and whether or not the outcomes were ethical. Bring in an expert who will assess the students on their interpretations.

Simulation of real decision-making. In a particular field (e.g., stock market) provide students with a simulation in which they act as an 'expert' who must make decisions (e.g., buying or selling stocks) that have real costs. Students should identify what outcomes they were striving for, how successful they were at achieving them, what side effects they created, and how they would change their behavior next time.

Participating in social justice activities. Have students find out what has happened and is happening in the community. Students then think of a social justice action that they can participate in within their community. What outcome do they want to see as a result of their social justice action? What are the steps they need to take to reach the goal? Who needs to be involved in the process? What do they need to succeed? Help students plan and implement their decision.

Starred ★ activities within each subskill go together!

Assessment Hints

Reasoning about actions and outcomes

Use multiple-choice, true-false, short answer, or essay tests to assess students' understanding of certain standards (e.g., fairness, benevolence, loyalty, etc.) and the likely or common outcomes of each standard.

Present new ethical dilemmas to students and have students list the possible actions to be taken in the dilemma, the standards of reasoning to be used for each action, and the possible outcomes for each action.

Present different dilemmas based on different standards (e.g., fairness, benevolence, loyalty, etc.) and have students identify what standards apply to each dilemma and what outcomes could occur for each applied standard.

Create a Climate
to Develop Ethical Reasoning

- Encourage students to use ethical reasoning to make decisions.

- Encourage students to carefully and systematically think about a social problem and consciously use a decision-making process to make ethical decisions.

- Encourage students to discuss ethical decisions with their parents and elders.

- Remind students that their decisions affect family, school, neighborhood, and community.

- Encourage students' commitment to justice/fairness through discussing students' experiences of injustice, reading about leaders for social justice, or performing a social justice action in the community.

- Encourage students' commitment to be impartial throughout the judgment process. Discuss human tendencies to favor one individual over another, or not consider all options, or misjudge the probability of consequences occurring. Discuss with them human tendencies to lose control and do harm when emotions are high.

Sample Student Self-Monitoring
Developing Ethical Reasoning

Encourage active learning by having students learn to monitor their own learning

Judging perspectives

Am I thinking carefully about the problem and my reasons?
Do I know what my biases are?
What biases do I have that would affect my decision?
Do I know how my biases affect my decision-making process?
Am I considering others' perspectives?

Reasoning about standards and ideals

What would be the most just or fair decision, based on standards and ideals?
How do my obligations and commitments affect my decision?
Am I objectively prioritizing my ethical ideals, standards, and the outcomes?

Reasoning about actions and outcomes

Do I know what all of the consequences would be?
Am I considering all of the consequences?
How do I want others to be affected by my decision?
What would be the most just or fair decision, based on the outcomes?
Am I objectively prioritizing my ethical ideals, standards, and the outcomes?

Understanding
Ethical Problems
(Analyze the Situation)

Ethical
Judgment 3

WHAT

Understanding problems is one of the first steps in any problem-solving and decision-making process. It is a step that students tend to ignore. To fully understand a problem, regardless of the subject area, a person must correctly define the problem and determine what information is important and what is irrelevant. The problem solver gathers the information needed from credible sources. The problem solver organizes the important information in order to generate options and strategies for solving the problem.

WHY

Understanding is one of the first steps of any problem-solving and decision-making process (Bransford & Stein, 1984; Marzano, 1988). The ability to understand a problem is important because it

- determines the types of solutions considered and determined (Sternberg, 1981),
- is necessary for effective decision making (Wheeler & Janis, 1980), and
- facilitates a student's generalization to new problems with different content (Ellis & Siegler, 1994).

Understanding ethical problems is one of the steps in problem solving and decision making that students tend to ignore (Bransford, Sherwood, Rieser, & Vye, 1986); therefore, it needs to be emphasized.

EJ-3 Understanding Ethical Problems

Web Wise
Find interactive lessons at www.webquest.org
Teach for Understanding materials to help teachers: http://learnweb.harvard.edu/alps/tfu/design.cfm
Learn to question and think skeptically: http://skepdic.com/contents.html
A website that encourages action against misleading commercials: http://www.commercialalert.org

SUBSKILLS OVERVIEW

1: Gathering information
- Judging the credibility of sources
- Distinguishing fact from opinion
- Getting enough of the *right* information

2: Analyzing ethical problems
- Dilemmas (one value against another)
- Ethical failure (lack of ethical sensitivity, judgment, motivation,implementation)
- Outward form vs. fundamental value (the same fundamental value expressed in different ways vs. clash of fundamentally different values)
- Who, what, where, when, how, why

Note: Developmental differences exist in determining "what" the problem is. Identifying the main idea or conflict in the problem is dependent upon students' abstract thinking skills and on students' past experiences. As students develop more complex cognitive skills and as students acquire more diverse, positive experiences, their definition of what the problem is will be more elaborate and their understanding of the problem will deepen.

Understanding Ethical Problems by Gathering Information

Koki Roberts is known for excellent political journalism. She is an expert in locating the right kind of information and judging the credibility of the sources of the information she uses.

Level 1: Immersion in Examples and Opportunities
Attend to the big picture, Learn to recognize basic patterns

Thinking about social problems. Discuss with students the importance of gathering information about the problem/issue in order to understand what the problem is. Present a problem to the class (e.g., homelessness, animal rights, etc.) and brainstorm (1) what additional information they would want to gather about the problem, and (2) where one could get that information (e.g., newspapers, internet, homeless shelters).

Thinking about a problem in the community. Use a problem that exists in your own community (e.g., vandalism, social isolation among the elderly). Briefly present the problem to students (or have them identify and present the problem). Have them (1) discuss what additional information they would like to gather about this problem in order to better understand it and (2) brainstorm where they might be able to obtain the information.

Gathering information in a particular subject area. Invite community members from different fields to discuss what kinds of information they gather to make good decisions. Have students take notes and find commonalities among them.

Gathering information at work. Have students interview and/or watch an adult at work and find out what kinds of information are collected and used to make decisions. Are the kinds of information collected different for different decisions?

Getting enough information. Present examples of situations where participants did not have enough information and made a bad decision. Examples could include accidentally firing at allies in war ("friendly fire") or using chlorofluorocarbons to refrigerate air and not knowing that they damage the ozone.

Level 2: Attention to Facts and Skills
Focus on detail and prototypical examples, Build knowledge

Distinguish facts from feelings/opinions. Present students with a lengthy description of a dilemma (e.g., drilling for oil on public park land, modifying buildings for the disabled) and have them list the facts of the situation and the feelings and opinions of people involved in the dilemma. You may also use periodicals, stories, novels, television, film.

Starred ⭐ activitie within each subskill go together!

Understanding Ethical Problems by Gathering Information
Ideas for Developing Skills

Level 2 (continued)

Newspaper fact or opinion? Have students bring in newspaper articles that interest them (you might specify which sections of the paper from which to draw and allow them to bring more than one). Discuss the viewpoints presented: which are facts (e.g., one car hit another car) and which are opinions (let's raise taxes to pay for new school buildings). On what are the opinions based (e.g., good reasoning, emotion, self-interest, civic mindedness)?

Credibility of sources. Using one of the larger problems from the Level 1 activity (e.g., homelessness, animal rights). Present example information from the various sources that students identified (e.g., newspapers, internet). Discuss the credibility of the sources. Which sources are appropriate for what kind of information? Would some sources be more likely to have information that is based more on their opinions rather than on the facts of the problem?

Determining the credibility of information in ads. Discuss with students how information presented in media ads may be skewed or biased in order to better sell their product. For example, ads for over-the-counter drug don't always list side effects, or may diminish side effects. Have students find ads in magazines, newspapers, and television that appear biased. Have students present them to the class, explaining how they appear biased or are skewing information.

Hearing from an expert in gathering information. Bring in a journalist or researcher to discuss the importance of "getting their facts straight," possibly using examples of when they didn't get their facts straight and what the consequences were. Have the journalist discuss how he or she determines credibility of a source and distinguishes fact from opinion.

Gathering information for a community problem/class project. Have students gather information from multiple sources as part of a class project (e.g., using the community problem from the starred Level 1 activity as a class project). Discuss with students the following aspects of information gathering: "Where can they get information about the problem/issue/topic?" "Do they need to know any special procedures/processes to get the information?" "Who can help them obtain more information or give advice about where and how to get it (e.g., local person familiar with the community problem, a librarian)?"

Tune up your observation skills. (1) One of the best ways to sharpen observation skills is by learning to draw. Edwards' *Drawing on the Right Side of the Brain* encourages drawing the spaces and shadows of what we see. This requires us to really <u>look</u> and really <u>see</u>, prerequisites for good drawing. (For more information: http://www.dharma-haven.org/five-havens/drawing.htm.) Have students try this for a week or more. (2) Have the group of students sit in one place (e.g., outside) and write down everything they see. Then compare lists. Keep trying this until everyone has virtually identical (long) lists.

Starred ★ activities within each subskill go together!

Understanding Ethical Problems by Gathering Information
Ideas for Developing Skills

Level 3: Practice Procedures
Set goals, Plan steps of problem solving, Practice skills

Judging the credibility of media sources. Have students look critically at media sources. Discuss the following questions with them: "Is the source objective, as good news sources should be?" "What does the media source want you to think?" "What does the source assume you like and your goals are?" "How does the source entice you?" "How credible is the source?" "How real is the issue/problem/situation/topic depicted in the media source?" Other discussions you may want to have with this activity:

- Identify areas where the media pressures students (look at television shows, magazine articles, music videos and songs, movies, video games, etc.).
- Define media pressure (look at the subtle messages that the media say about who you should be, how you should look, how you should act, what is beautiful, what is success, what you should focus your life on, what you should do with your time, what you should think of your peers, what you should think of adults, etc.).
- Discuss typical portrayals that media present and why they might have so much power.

Practicing journalism skills. Discuss with students two important skills that journalists have: (1) determining that the source of information is credible, and (2) distinguishing facts from opinion. Present a controversial news event to the class and practice the skills. **Assess** by having students write a report on a news event to practice these skills on their own. They could either all report on the same event or each choose their own.

Evaluating information sources on a social problem. Have students select a difficult social problem that interests them. Have them gather information on it and report on their sources. They should have answers to questions regarding the credibility of the source and the certainty of the credibility.

Evaluating gathered information for a community problem/class project. Have students gather information about a community problem or class project. Have them organize the information and discuss how they determine whether they have enough information. Did they find information representing all viewpoints? Once all the information is gathered, have students determine whether they gathered any conflicting information, and have them evaluate which sources may be more credible than others.

EJ-3 Understanding Ethical Problems

Starred ★ activities
within each subskill
go together!

Understanding Ethical Problems by Gathering Information
Ideas for Developing Skills

Level 4: Integrate Knowledge and Procedures
Execute plans, Solve problems

★ **Articulating the gathered information for a community problem/class project.** Once students have gathered information about the community problem or class project and evaluated it, have them write a detailed description of the problem (and/or present it to the class) using the information from sources they determined most credible, making sure to represent multiple viewpoints. Have them present their ideas to a local community.

Assessment Hints

Gathering Information

Use multiple-choice, true-false, short answer, or essay tests to assess students' knowledge of gathering information skills (e.g., assessing the credibility of sources, distinguishing fact from opinion, and getting enough and the right information from multiple viewpoints).

Use news clips or written scenarios and have students distinguish the facts from opinions, evaluate the credibility of the source, and assess whether there has been enough information gathered.

Use a dilemma (written or video clip) and have students distinguish the facts from opinions.

Starred ★ activities within each subskill go together!

Understanding Ethical Problems by Analyzing Them

As National Security Advisor, **Condoleezza Rice** is an expert in categorizing problems. Ms. Rice must excel in this skill in order to understand problems in other areas of the world, particularly in Afghanistan and the Middle East.

Creative and Expert Implementer Real-Life Example

Ideas for Developing Skills

Level 1: Immersion in Examples and Opportunities
Attend to the big picture, Learn to recognize basic patterns

Identifying ethical and non-ethical problems. Present a set of problems to students (e.g., what to wear, what to do when you're mad at a friend; what to do with your garbage when you are finished with a picnic, etc.). Discuss with students the distinction between ethical (how to get along with others) and non-ethical problems. Have students think about examples of each and discuss them. Present a range of ethical problems, from the simple to the more complex, emphasizing the importance of being able to understand the complexity of an ethical problem before making a judgment or decision. For example, what are ethical problems for a toddler or a first grade student? What are ethical problems for middle school students? For high school and college students? For parents? For teachers? For presidents? **Assess**: Give students multiple dilemmas, both ethical and non-ethical. Ask the students to identify which dilemmas are ethical and which are nonethical.

Different ways to categorize ethical problems. Present to students examples of the different ways to categorize ethical problems, focusing on the type most relevant to your subject matter. There are multiple ways to categorize ethical problems, for example: (a) by type of ethical failure (see the chart on p. 85), (b) by type of ethical decision (e.g., equal access to voting is a matter of justice and human rights, not of beneficence), (c) by type of ethical outcome (e.g., what to do with an abused child: temporarily get them out of the home, put them in foster care for the short-term, rehabilitate parents for the long-term), (d) by whom is affected by the problem (e.g., burning leaves in my backyard: I'm polluting the air I breathe, the air my neighbors breathe, the atmosphere generally, worsening global pollution; eating a high-fat diet: I am hurting my chances for a long life, and affecting the welfare of my loved ones), (e) by sphere (e.g., whether to save the life of a very premature disabled fetus: biomedically it is possible, sociopolitically it costs the taxpayers for as long as the child lives, personally the parents pay monetarily, emotionally, and timewise), (f) by content (e.g., punishing the whole class to get the guilty party to confess is a violation of due process for the innocent children, not an issue of confidentiality, not an issue of presenting fairly and fully the subject matter).

Clear Non-Ethical Problems
What kind of soft drink to buy
What color shirt to wear
What book to read first
What kind of pillow you use

Clear Ethical Problems
What to do when someone insults you
What to do when your best friends gossips about you
Cheating on a test to get a good grade
Taking something that isn't yours

Are these Ethical Problems?
Whether or not to use tobacco
What classes to take
Taking long showers
How much time you spend playing video or computer games
How much time you spend talking on the phone
What to do after school
What to do with garbage when there is no waste receptacle

EJ-3 Understanding Ethical Problems

Starred activities within each subskill go together!

Understanding Ethical Problems by Analyzing Them
Ideas for Developing Skills

Level 1 (continued)

What Is Ethical Failure?

Lack of ethical sensitivity:
lack of awareness of (1) how our actions affect other people, (2) multiple lines of action, (3) consequences of possible actions; poor empathy and role-taking skills
<u>Example</u>: a student makes fun of another student's clothes because they are not the fashions others kids wear

Lack of ethical judgment:
simplistic ways of justifying choices of ethical action
<u>Example</u>: Mark justifies stealing Joe's jacket because Joe left his jacket in the locker room

Lack of ethical motivation:
prioritizing non-ethical values over ethical values
<u>Example</u>: Sheila, not wanting to be labeled as a "rat," does not tell school officials that her friend was the one who called in the bomb threat that morning

Lack of ethical action:
lack of implementation skills (e.g., communication, conflict resolution, assertiveness skills) and easy discouragement to follow through on the action
<u>Example</u>: Todd witnessed another student being bullied by a group of students but he doesn't know what to do to stop it

Finding ethical problems and identifying the important information. Have students find ethical problems in newspapers, journals, and television news shows and write a description of the problem in their own words. Have students share their descriptions. Point out the critical information that is needed to understand the problem: the who, what, when, where, and why.

Level 2: Attention to Facts and Skills
Focus on detail and prototypical examples, Build knowledge

Clashing Values. Discuss what should be done in the following dilemmas (or others you see your students struggle with) and what values are clashing. You may use one of the formats in the Ethical Dilemma Discussion method in the appendix. (1) You promised to babysit/mow a lawn on Saturday (and you need the money) but your friend has invited you to the lake for the day (and you are dying to go). (2) You saw one of your neighbors take another neighbor's bicycle. Without a bicycle the neighbor can't get to work, except to take a 2-hour bus ride each way, but the neighbor has other responsibilities scheduled for those two hours. (3) Use a real-life classroom-based conflict, if appropriate. (4) Use a values conflict from a newspaper story or literature.

Understanding ethical failure. Identify or have students identify instances of ethical failure. Analyze, using the ethical process model, what might have gone wrong. See "What Is Ethical Failure?" chart on left for definitions and examples.

Ethical failure in stories. Select a subset from the "Examples of Ethical Failures" list on page 85. Select materials (book excerpts, videos, etc.) that illustrate each of the failures you have selected. Have students match the excerpt to the failure. Discuss how the character could have acted differently to avoid failure.

Same values shown differently. Discuss with students how many people have the same values but show them differently. For example, the value of showing respect when meeting someone can vary from culture to culture. In some cultures you shake hands and look people in the eye; another culture you hug and kiss; in others you bow. The fundamental value is showing respect to a newly introduced person, but the outward form, or behavior, varies. Many times these different behaviors can lead to problems and conflicts if the people are not aware that they are expressing the same value in different forms. Find examples of misunderstandings in your community that are based on different forms of expressing the same value.

Starred ★ activities within each subskill go together!

Examples of Ethical Failures

Ethical Sensitivity

Perspectives
Not expressing emotions
Not taking another's perspective
Not taking a particular cultural perspective
Not taking the perspective of the less fortunate
Unable to determine what is happening
Unable to deal with ambiguity
Not responding creatively
Ethnocentrism
Social bias

Connection to others
Poorly relating to others
Not showing care
Unfriendliness
Emotionally erratic
Mismanaging anger or aggression
Miscommunicating
Imbalance between unity and diversity in the community

Ethical Motivation

Irreverence
Disrespecting others
Disrespecting self
Incivility
Disrespecting the natural world
Poor stewardship
Not valuing traditions
Misunderstanding social structures
Lack of purpose in life
Not focused
No commitment
Ignoring aesthetics
Choosing evil
Not creating an ethical identity

Pride
Intemperate use of influence and power
Dishonorable behavior
Holding grudges
Not meeting obligations
Disregard of global citizenship
Not helping others
Acting unthoughtfully towards others
Hoarding or not sharing resources
Negatively influencing others
Not reaching potential

Ethical Judgment

Reasoning
Not reasoning objectively
Using faulty reasoning
Human reasoning pitfall
Misjudging perspectives
Misjudging outcomes
Not gathering enough or the right information
Miscategorizing the problem
Not reasoning about means and ends
Making wrong choices
Not reflecting or monitoring one's reasoning
Mischaracterizing applicable code
Misunderstanding which code to apply
Not attending to consequences
Applying negative reasoning in social situations
Failing to modify affect in thinking
Mismanaging disappointment and failure

Ethical Action

Misaction
Not resolving conflicts and problems
Not negotiating
Not balancing the common good and individual excellence
Using violence
Not attending to human needs
Not using appropriate rhetoric
Not balancing submission and assertiveness
Not taking initiative as a leader
Poor leadership skills
Not taking initiative for others
Making poor decisions for the group
Not thinking strategically
Poor planning
Not planning resource use

Not following through
Not managing fear
Collapsing under pressure
Not knowing when to change
Giving up too soon
Not overcoming obstacles
Not pushing oneself
Not working hard enough
Not balancing being thorough with avoiding perfectionism
Setting unreachable goals
Mismanaging time

Understanding Ethical Problems by Analyzing Them
Ideas for Developing Skills

Level 2 (continued)

Identifying critical elements in personal stories. (1) Have a community member come to class (high school student or young adult) who tells a personal story with an ethical dilemma embedded in it. The community member describes the problem's critical elements. Afterwards, in groups, students summarize the dilemma by identifying who was involved in the dilemma, when and where it took place and into which kind of ethical problem category it fits. (2) Do the same activity with an example from a book or film/show.

Perspective taking of characters/groups in conflict. Have students watch a film or read a book about a conflict. Facilitate a class discussion about what kind of ethical problem it was, and what kind of ethical failure occurred (or could have occurred).

Seeing different sides of the problem. (1) Present to the students a well-described dilemma that contains multiple perspectives of what the dilemma is. Discuss with the students the multiple perspectives of the dilemma, and compare and contrast these perspectives. Help them identify what all of the perspectives are and why it's important to know them all. (2) Bring in at least two visitors with different perspectives on a problem. Ask the visitors to help the students understand their particular perspectives. (3) Use a salient dispute in the community or school and have student groups try to outline the different perspectives.

Defining the problem or issue in news articles. Collect news articles, and with the class, define the conflict within a few news articles. Have students practice defining the problem of other news articles in small groups in which they are to identify and record the main idea/conflict presented in the article.

Defining the main conflict in stories/plots. Discuss with students how almost all literature, movies, and television shows are about a conflict. Using literature, movies, or television shows, students determine the main conflict.

Making visual maps of problems. Present a description of a problem to the class, preferably a problem in the community (such as the one students work on in the starred activities in Subskill 1). Have the students make a visual map of the problem, answering the following questions: What is the problem? Who is involved in the problem? What are the perspectives of each party involved? Where is the problem occurring? When is the problem occurring? When does the problem have to be resolved? Encourage the students to be creative in how they visually represent the problem. **Assess** students' visual map of the problem for accuracy, completeness, and creativity.

Starred ★ activities within each subskill go together!

Understanding Ethical Problems
by Analyzing Them
Ideas for Developing Skills

Level 3: Practice Procedures
Set goals, Plan steps of problem solving, Practice skills

Interviewing elders about different types of ethical problems. Review the different ways that ethical problems can be categorized (Level 2 activities of clashing values, failure of ethical processes, expressing different forms of the same value). Have students think of questions they could ask an elder (family or community member) about each of these categories. Students then interview the elder and report back to class.

Categorizing ethical problems in media stories. Review the different ways that ethical problems can be categorized (e.g., the Level 2 activities of clashing values, failure of ethical processes, expressing different forms of the same value). Have students find an example of one (or each) of these in the media and present it to the class.

What's an ethical decision? (1) Help students distinguish between problems that can be solved with few consequences to people and other life forms (e.g., what color to paint the school) and problems that affect people and other life forms directly or indirectly. (2) Help students distinguish between ethical issues (those that bear on the welfare of people) and non-ethical or neutral issues (those that don't). Have student groups examine a periodical and make a list of each kind of choice/issue reflected in the periodical. Discuss findings with whole class. (3) There are different perspectives as to what the definition of an ethical decision is. For example, most adults think using drugs is an unethical action whereas many young people reason that using drugs is a personal affair. Have students generate a list of issues they think are ethical and ones that they face that they believe are not ethical decisions (see chart on p. 83 for examples). Have them interview other students and adults to see if they agree. Present and discuss results with class. **Assess** with a set of problems that they must categorize as ethical issues or not and explain why.

Comparing problems to better understand them. Design a set of problems (see samples at right) that you think would interest the students and put each on an index card. Put the cards in a basket and have students each draw one. Have them think about their problem and write some thoughts using a decision-making model. Then have them discuss it with a small group or the large group. As a follow-up activity, review the same problems and discuss these questions: Are there problems that are similar to the problem posed? How is the similar problem the same as the present one? How is the similar problem different than the present one? Is there any information from the similar problem that can provide insights to understanding the present problem?

Starred ★ activities within each subskill go together!

Sample problems:
- Curfew for an 8-year-old compared to a curfew for a 14-year-old
- Taking music off the web without paying vs. shoplifting from a store
- Not telling the truth about cheating vs. not telling the truth about your friend's bad haircut
- Failing a promise to watch a friend's pet vs. failing a promise to watch your friend's favorite TV show so you can tell them what happened after they return from out of town

EJ-3 Understanding Ethical Problems

Understanding Ethical Problems by Analyzing Them
Ideas for Developing Skills

Level 3 (continued)

Culture clashes. Find examples of situations where cultures clash. Determine which clashes are based on different values (e.g., loyalty to family vs. individual independence) and which are based on disagreement about how the underlying value is expressed (e.g., respect to elders shown by looking elder in the eye vs. holding head down and not looking directly at elder). In some culture clashes the underlying values may not be easily identifiable unless one has substantial knowledge about the culture. Discuss with students the importance of having enough information about the cultures to appropriately understand the cultural clash.

National and international conflicts. Have students find examples of national and international conflicts, from large to small. Ask them to explain what the conflict is about and analyze the kinds of problems involved. Working on other skills, have students determine a course of action to share their ideas for solving the issue with the parties involved.

Understanding conflicts and parties' goals. Discuss with students how many conflicts in ethical problems involve individuals or groups having different goals, needs, and assumptions. Present examples of such conflicts to the class and have them discuss each party's goals, needs, and assumptions in resolving the problem for each example.

Analyzing embedded dilemmas in readings. Have students read a story (Literature or Social Studies reading) with an ethical dilemma embedded in it. Help the students define the dilemma by answering any or all of the following: what the problem is, who is involved, and what the parties' goals are.

Identifying biases in social problems. Have the students practice identifying their own and others' biases in describing specific social problems.

Identifying biases in a community problem. Have the students identify their own and others' possible biases in describing the community problem in the starred Level 2 activity.

Starred ★ activities
within each subskill
go together!

Understanding Ethical Problems
by Analyzing Them
Ideas for Developing Skills

Level 4: Integrate Knowledge and Procedures
Execute plans, Solve problems

Tracking problems. Have students keep a journal for a week in which they record problems and conflicts they come across in television shows, movies, books, at school, family, and personally (minimum of 3 per day). Have students categorize each one according to whether it is ethical or not and explain why they think it fits there.

Understanding why a problem is occurring. In order to understand why a problem is occurring, students must be able to correctly identify what the problem is, who the parties are and what their goals are, how the problem came to be, and when and where the problem is occurring. Have students choose one problem that interests them (a list of ideas is given below, or using the community problem from the starred activities in Levels 2 and 3) and write a report detailing what the problem is and speculating about why it is occurring.

Example problems to write about:
- Children not getting enough to eat
- Global warming
- Illiteracy
- Voter registration

Assessment Hints

Analyzing Ethical Problems

Use a set of problems, both ethical and non-ethical, and have students identify which ones are ethical problems and why.

Use multiple choice, true-false, short answer, or essay tests to assess students' knowledge of categorizing problems and knowledge of problem analysis (e.g., what the problem is, who is involved, and what their perspectives and goals are, where and when the problem is occurring).

Use news clips or written scenarios and have students categorize the problem: clashing values (which values?), ethical failure (what kind?), outward form of the same value (which value?).

Present a new problem to the students and have them analyze it in a short answer or essay question.

EJ-3 Understanding Ethical Problems

Starred ★ activities within each subskill go together!

Understanding Ethical Problems by Making Moral Judgments

Creative and Expert Implementer Real-Life Example

Bobby Lunsford dedicated much of his time understanding an ethical problem at his job and made an important moral judgment. As a research lab technician at the University of Missouri, he discovered that he, his coworkers, and children at a nearby school were being exposed to dangerously high levels of lead. Mr. Lunsford talked to his supervisors about this problem who subsequently denied it and transferred him to another position. Mr. Lunsford further examined the problem on his own to better understand it and then contacted federal authorities who are now resolving it.

Ideas for Developing Skills

Level 1: Immersion in Examples and Opportunities
Attend to the big picture, Learn to recognize basic patterns

Making moral judgments about motives and actions. Present a video, film or story to the students and ask them to judge the actions and motives of the characters.

Noticing moral actions. A moral action is one that is intended to bring about more good. Present to students a video, film, or story and ask them to judge which character brought about more good (i.e., which character was the most moral).

Local community examples of moral judgments. Bring in local leaders as guest speakers and ask them to discuss the decision-making process for some key local issues/problems. Have students write a response to the leader with follow-up questions.

Level 2: Attention to Facts and Skills
Focus on detail and prototypical examples, Build knowledge

Making moral judgments in the professions. Select examples from a particular field to read about and discuss. After gathering information and analyzing the problem, discuss whether the morally-right choice was made. Sample professions and examples of situations to discuss follow. (1) Science: (a) study the Manhattan project (deciding to make the atomic bomb). (2) Engineering: (a) study the evolution of refrigeration and how freon (chlorofluorocarbons) was selected because it did not explode but was subsequently found out to destroy the ozone layer in the atmosphere; (b) study the decision-making process in genetic engineering. (3) Business: (a) study the incident of recalling Tylenol from all store shelves due to tampering found on a couple of bottles (b) study examples of business leaders who put their workers first, over profit; (c) study immoral decision makers such as those within the tobacco industry.

Starred ★ activities within each subskill go together!

Understanding Ethical Problems by Making Moral Judgments
Ideas for Developing Skills

Level 2 (continued)

Making moral judgments about social life. Select examples from a social arena to read about and discuss. After gathering information and analyzing the problem, discuss the reasons for the choices that were made and whether the right choice was made. (1) Historic civic life: (a) African-American slavery, (b) women's right to vote, (c) children's rights. (2) Personal social life: (a) drug use, (b) pre-marital sex, (c) how you focus your time and energy, (d) how you spend your money.

Level 3: Practice Procedures
Set goals, Plan steps of problem solving, Practice skills

Work with community. Find issues of current concern in the community. Have students interview multiple community members with different perspectives about the issues and about what they think is the moral judgment that should be made. Students synthesize what they found in a report to class.

Reenactments of history and literature. Find examples in which characters or historic figures made bad decisions. Have students rewrite stories in which the person makes a good decision. Select the best essays and reenact the critical scenes in the original form and in the revised.

Level 4: Integrate Knowledge and Procedures
Execute plans, Solve problems

Problem solving: Making moral judgments in particular fields.
Select some current issues/problems in a particular field. Have students gather information, analyze the problem, and then debate the issues, advocating one decision or another. Have experts evaluate the students' argumentation for completeness. Current issues might include: (1) Science and engineering: (a) cloning, (b) stem cell research, (c) energy sources; (2) Business: (a) moving headquarters out of the country to avoid paying taxes, (b) having a product's parts produced in different parts of the world, including in countries with whom we don't have solid positive relations, (c) regulation of manufacturing pollution and contamination; (3) Fine arts: (a) taxing citizens to support public theatre, (b) cutting music programs in public schools when budgets get tight; (4) Sport: (a) signing multimillion dollar contracts with athletes, (b) moving sport teams if the public doesn't build a new stadium, (c) allowing cheating to occur (e.g., in non-tournament tennis matches); (5) Medicine: (a) making citizens pay for their own health care, (b) not selling human organs on the open market.

Assessment Hints

Making moral judgments

In a particular domain, test students with common domain moral problems.

Have students write an essay about a person who made a significant moral judgment, describing the problem and their decision.

Students rotate leadership of class decision-making.

EJ-3 Understanding Ethical Problems

Starred ★ activities within each subskill go together!

Create a Climate
to Help Students Better Understand Ethical Problems

- Encourage students to be optimistic about being able to understand and solve ethical problems. Model this optimism as well.
- Encourage students to carefully and systematically think about a problem.

Sample Student Self-Monitoring
Understanding Ethical Problems

Encourage active learning by having students learn to monitor their own learning

Gathering Information

Do I know how to identify what information I need to solve the problem?

Is the information I have about the problem fact or opinion?

Is the information about the problem that I have unbiased and accurate? If information is biased, do I have information with an opposite bias?

Do I have enough information about the problem?

Analyzing Ethical Problems

Are there clashing values in this dilemma? If yes, what are they?

Is this problem due to a lack of ethical sensitivity, judgment, motivation, or implementation?

Is this a problem of the same value being expressed in different ways? What value is it? How is it being expressed differently?

Did I identify all the people involved in the problem?

Did I identify when the problem is occurring?

Did I identify where the problem is occurring?

Did I identify the central issue of the problem?

Do I know what my goal is in this problem?

Do I know what other people's goals are that are involved in this problem?

Do I understand the perspectives of the other people that are involved in this problem?

Do I understand why the problem is occurring?

Making Moral Judgments

I try to make decisions that lead to the most good in the world.

I make amends when I made poor moral judgments.

Selections to Post in the Classroom
For Understanding Problems

PROBLEM-SOLVING STEPS
(adapted from Bransford & Stein, 1984)

1. Identify the problem.
2. Define the problem.
3. Explore strategies for solving the problem (break problem into sub-problems).
4. Look for potential biases (e.g. ideological blindness).
5. Make plans for solving the problem.
6. Take action.
7. Look for the effects of your action.

Good problem solvers go through each step. Poor ones jump to 5.

Ethical Judgment 4

Using Codes & Identifying Judgment Criteria

(Know rules and practices)

WHAT

Codes are what we know and use to act respectfully and responsibly in different domains or contexts. The different sources of codes include explicit and implicit rules and laws and ethical standards, which may vary from one context to the next. Contexts may be more local, such as school, family, and work, or broader, such as national and international.

WHY

Students need to know different sets of codes and be able to apply them in the appropriate context. Applying the appropriate sets of codes in different contexts is a necessary element of ethical reasoning and is important in acting prosocially (Oliner & Oliner, 1988). Also, valuing and appropriately applying codes is important for practicing good citizenship.

SUBSKILLS OVERVIEW

Characterizing codes
Discerning code application
Judging code validity

Web Wise

Lesson plans about peace, war, conflict at www.esrnational.org

See lesson plans and information at the The Institute for Global Ethics: http://www.globalethics.org/EDS/default.html

Using Codes
by Characterizing Them

Kofi Anan, the UN Secretary General of several years, leads nations toward peaceful coexistence. In order to perform his job well, he needs to be able to adjust to different rules and codes in the many countries he visits around the world.

Creative and Expert Implementer Real-Life Example

Ideas for Developing Skills

Level 1: Immersion in Examples and Opportunities
Attend to the big picture, Learn to recognize basic patterns

Unspoken codes in varying contexts. Bring to students' attention that most codes are unspoken (what "feels right") and vary across different contexts. Examples include: (1) implicit dress codes for formal events (e.g., symphony concerts, funeral) and informal events (e.g., football game, beach party) and (2) how students refer to teachers/principal (Mr./Ms./Mrs. Last Name) and friends (first name only). Present film clips from movies about people from another time or place visiting the US now. Discuss with students what they might do if they were unsure of implicit codes in a situation (would they watch others? ask someone else? who would they ask?). ★

Level 2: Attention to Facts and Skills
Focus on detail and prototypical examples, Build knowledge

Exploring family codes. (1) <u>Exploring codes in different contexts</u>. Have students explore their family codes or rules in various contexts. Ask them to be objective observers of their family's culture (in other words, ethnographic researchers). *Possible contexts*: Eating a meal together at home, going out to eat, watching television, holiday gatherings with relatives. Possible questions to explore (example using eating dinner together as a family): What kind of behavior is expected (no singing at the dinner table, no elbows)? How are you expected to be groomed (clean hands to eat, combed hair, shirt and shoes)? What is the order of events (first we pray, then we pass the food around until everyone is served, then we all pick up our forks and eat)? What actions do people have to take (pray before eating)? What roles do people play (Dad always says the prayer)? What kinds of things can you say or talk about (we talk about current events)? What things can't you do or say (no swearing, no games at the table)? How do things start (Mom calls us to eat)? How do they end (unless you have cleanup duty, when you are finished you ask to be excused from the table)? (2) <u>Comparing codes.</u> Have the students share their codes for one activity and note the family differences. (3) <u>Cultural differences.</u> Through research or interviews of community members from different cultures, have students find examples of people who have different codes for the same activities.

Starred ★ activities within each subskill go together!

Using Codes
by Characterizing Them
Ideas for Developing Skills

Level 2 (continued)

Exploring school codes. (1) With a uniform set of questions, have students find out about their school code from different members of the community (one student interviews the custodian; one interviews a cook, etc.). Students report and compare notes. (2) With a uniform set of questions, have the students explore the codes at other contemporary schools by interviewing students and staff from other schools nearby. (3) With a uniform set of questions, have the students explore the codes at other schools historically by interviewing their elders or older siblings about their experiences in the same grade.

Exploring community codes: public behavior. Have students interview different community members about appropriate behaviors in particular public/community locations. First all students interview their families, next their neighbors, then business folk, then politicians, etc. Students collect the information in a binder and compare across interviewee categories. Community contexts: playground/park, stores, street, etc.

Community member work codes. Have students interview community members who work in different domains (hospital, grocery store, day care) about the different codes of each interviewee in their work and how the interviewees apply them. Ask students write a report of their interview and/or present it to the class.

Level 3: Practice Procedures
Set goals, Plan steps of problem solving, Practice skills

Exploring citizenship codes. (1) Have students interview different community members about citizenship. Students collect the information in a binder and compare across interviewee category. (2) Facilitate discussion among the students on what it means to be a good citizen in your community (e.g. respecting and having concern for others, being of service to their community, taking personal responsibility for their actions and intentions). (3) Have students compare and contrast their results from the Level 2 activity ("Exploring community codes") to this activity. What are the similarities and differences in the codes that the community members discussed for public behavior codes and citizenship codes? How much do they overlap? Are there any codes unique to citizenship? (4) Read essays by other students about what it means to be a good citizen, then have students write an essay on their conceptions of citizenship.

Starred ★ activities
within each subskill
go together!

Using Codes
by Characterizing Them
Ideas for Developing Skills

Level 3 (continued)

Citizenship differences. In lessons on specific countries, discuss with students the differences in what citizenship means in different countries and under different political/social systems. Ask students to describe how they could be good citizens if they were living in that country.

Exploring school codes in other countries. (1) Have students communicate with students in another country to find out about the school codes there (if possible, have students from more than one country communicate with your students). (2) Have guest speakers who are from (or are very familiar with) other countries talk to your class about the school codes in their country. Help the students come up with a specific set of questions to ask, and have students compile their responses into a written report.

Exploring international codes.
(1) <u>Consensus</u>. Have students read one or more of the documents listed below. Have them gather more information from the web or library and report on it. Invite experts to answer questions about the document and its impact.

    United Nations Declaration of Human Rights
    United Nations Declaration of the Rights of the Child
    Kyoto Global Warming agreement
    Nuclear Arms Test Ban Treaty

(2) <u>National Citizenship</u>. Conduct research on citizenship expectations in other countries (selected by student or teacher). Compare and constrast results with U.S. perspectives.

Future codes. Ask students what kinds of places they would like to go, activities they would like to do when they are adults, and have them find written sources about their codes, or interview someone familiar with the codes there. Have students write a report of their findings.

Level 4: Integrate Knowledge and Procedures
Execute plans, Solve problems

Code Mentor. Assign each of your students a younger child to mentor (kindergarten or first grade) in terms of helping the students learn school codes across contexts. Plan mentoring activities together that allow your students to "teach" school codes to the younger students.

Starred ★ activities
within each subskill
go together!

Assessment Hints

Characterizing codes

Give students a wide range of problems from multiple contexts (e.g., school, family, political, environmental) and ask them to describe the appropriate set of codes for each context, and if they don't know, have them list how they would find out.

Have students write a report on their interview findings and present the report to the class and hand it in to the teacher.

Give students an ethical dilemma that pertains to the social order and rules in the community, such as respect or responsibility. Ask the students to respond to it either in writing or by role playing how the person would respond. Questions for the students to answer include: (a) What codes would this person think applied to this problem? (b) How would the person use and apply each code to this problem? (c) Which code do you think should be used to solve the dilemma, and why? These can be contextualized by culture or location or time.

Ask students to write an essay on their conception of citizenship.

EJ-4 Using Codes and Identifying Judgment Criteria

Using Codes
by Discerning Code Application

When she was Secretary of State, **Madeleine Albright** had to learn a set of codes from many cultures and when and how to apply them. Ms. Albright had to excel in this skill in order to effectively communicate and negotiate with other countries.

Ideas for Developing Skills

Level 1: Immersion in Examples and Opportunities
Attend to the big picture, Learn to recognize basic patterns

Knowing and applying codes. Present to students film clips from movies about people from another time or place visiting the US now (e.g., *Coneheads, Coming to America*). Ask the students to identify which codes the character(s) is violating in the scenario. Ask if it is enough to only *know* the codes (versus knowing how to apply them). Have students discuss what code the characters should have applied.

International travelers. Invite to class several people who have lived in several different countries. Ask them to describe situations where they used a code from one culture in another culture with bad results.

Male-female code differences. Show clips from films or television shows in which male and female characters misunderstand one another due to different expectations or codes. Have students find other examples.

Level 2: Attention to Facts and Skills
Focus on detail and prototypical examples, Build knowledge

School codes in ethical dilemmas. Give students an ethical dilemma that pertains to the social order and rules of the school, such as respect or responsibility. Discuss with students what school codes apply to this dilemma. Questions for the students to answer include: (a) What codes apply to this problem? (b) When should [character A] use and apply each code to this problem (c) Which code do you think should be used to solve the dilemma, and why? Ask the students to role play the appropriate code.

Annotated checklists of codes in different contexts. Have students complete checklists of their own codes used in different contexts and explain why a particular code is appropriate for a particular context.

Starred activities within each subskill go together!

Using Codes
by Discerning Code Application
Ideas for Developing Skills

Level 3: Practice Procedures
Set goals, Plan steps of problem solving, Practice skills

Compare/contrast code applications. Ask students to write an essay on the codes that exist in two different contexts, in which they describe when they apply them and compare and contrast their applications. For example, codes at a basketball game and shopping mall: What are the codes and when and how are they applied? What are their similarities? What are their differences? Students can also interview family or community members about codes in two contexts that the students are not very familiar with, and then compare and contrast the interviewee responses about the codes.

Readings on citizenship codes. Have students read stories that involve citizenship issues (respect, responsibility, courtesy). Discuss with students what these issues mean and when and how to apply them in situations with strangers (at the grocery store, mall, concert).

Level 4: Integrate Knowledge and Procedures
Execute plans, Solve problems

Cultural variation of codes. Discuss with students how codes are often different in other cultures. For example, the behavioral codes when meeting someone new can vary from culture to culture. In some cultures you shake hands and look people in the eye; another culture you hug and kiss; in others you bow. Have students (individually or in groups) find examples of codes that vary by culture for the same situation and learn to do them. Encourage them to find examples of cultural variation of codes in the community if possible (using observation methods). Also, if possible, ask community members to assess how well the student can follow the codes and use them in the appropriate context. **Assess** by having students write reports of their findings or act out what they learned live or on videotape.

Starred ★ activities
within each subskill
go together!

Assessment Hints

Discerning code application

Give students a wide range of problems from multiple contexts (e.g., school, family, political, environmental) and ask them to describe the appropriate set of codes to each context, and how they should be applied.

Have students write an essay comparing and contrasting codes in two different contexts or cultures.

Give students an ethical dilemma that pertains to the social order and rules of the community, such as respect or responsibility. Ask the students to respond to it either in writing or by role playing how the person would respond. Questions for the students to answer include: (a) What codes would this person think applied to this problem? (b) How would the person use and apply each code to this problem? (c) Which code do you think should be used to solve the dilemma, and why? These can be contextualized by culture or location or time.

Ask students to write an essay on their conception of citizenship and how to apply their ideas of citizenship to a particular situation.

Using Codes
by Judging Code Validity

Confucius, the ancient Chinese philosopher and teacher, created and taught a comprehensive set of codes for humans. When Confucius was born, the Chinese government was going through many rapid changes, and many Chinese citizens no longer respected the established behavioral guidelines. Confucius brought back a set of codes through his philosophy and teachings. His ideas were the single strongest influence on Chinese society from around 100 BC to the AD 1900s. His philosophy still has much influence in Chinese society today as well as other societies around the world.

Ideas for Developing Skills

Level 1: Immersion in Examples and Opportunities
Attend to the big picture, Learn to recognize basic patterns

Necessity of classroom codes. Have students inteview a variety of people about (1) why classroom codes or rules are necessary, (2) what codes/rules the interviewer must follow each day, and (3) what would happen if the interviewer had no codes to follow. Have students interview about perspectives on school codes, public behavior codes in the community, and citizenship codes. Students report their findings.

Lord of the Flies. Read or watch *The Lord of the Flies* (Golding, 1962). Each time a decision about a rule is made, stop and discuss its validity.

Level 2: Attention to Facts and Skills
Focus on detail and prototypical examples, Build knowledge

Building classroom codes. Have the class collectively decide what classroom codes should be established. Ask students to justify each code as to why it should be used and enforced. Have students decide how the codes should be enforced (i.e., what should be done when codes are not followed). Afterwards, assist students in evaluating the codes they just created. Does each code have a purpose or reason for existing? How good is this reason? How will this code be implemented and enforced? Is the enforcement fair? You can also do this activity for school codes, public behavior codes in your community, and citizenship codes in which students hypothetically create their own ideal school/community.

Creative and Expert
Implementer
Real-Life Example

Starred activities
within each subskill
go together!

Using Codes
by Judging Code Validity
Ideas for Developing Skills

Level 2 (continued)

Historical codes that were unjust. Discuss the importance of changing codes that are unjust. Give examples such as slavery; Jim Crow laws that systematically discriminated, segregated and repressed blacks; women not being allowed to vote, get equal pay or have access to the same jobs as males. Discuss the economic, social and political consequences of these laws for the individuals, the groups, and the whole nation.

Historical comparison of codes. Select historical practices that contemporary societies think are vulgar or immoral. Compare the underlying codes that supported these practices. Compare with practices today. Discuss criteria for establishing and supporting a 'good' code (e.g., that it is fair, that all agree to it, that it is not harmful).

Finding codes. Have students investigate codes. Find codes for different organizations (via the internet or interviews with local community organizations) and compare them.

Sport and game codes. Identify different practices for a particular game or sport (e.g., football league differences: NFL, CFL, AFL). Discuss whether or not the different rules are valid codes. Discuss necessary features of a code (e.g., that it be fair, that all agree to it, that it is not harmful, or that it is traditional).

Level 3: Practice Procedures
Set goals, Plan steps of problem solving, Practice skills

Examples of conflicting codes in the community. Find examples of codes that conflict (or have conflicted) in community issues/problems. Discuss what the purpose is/may have been for the codes, whether the purpose was good, and how the conflict of codes could be or was resolved. Did the best codes prevail in the end? Were the means by which the codes "won" (e.g., protests, changes in laws, war) acceptable?

Historical examples of conflicting codes. In historical examples where codes conflict (e.g., Gandhi and the liberation of India), have students define what the conflicting codes are. Discuss what the purpose may have been for the codes, whether the purpose was good, and how the conflict of codes was resolved. Did the best codes prevail in the end? Were the means by which the codes "won" (e.g., protest, war) acceptable?

Challenging codes that are unjust. Have students find a code or law that they think is fair and just and to find one they think should be changed. They will need to research local ordinances, state and federal laws. (You might narrow the focus to a particular area of life.) Have students present the laws they chose and the rationale behind their opinion. They should use sound reasoning as described in the next skill, Reasoning Generally.

Starred 🌟 activities within each subskill go together!

EJ-4 Using Codes and Identifying Judgment Criteria

Using Codes
by Judging Code Validity
Ideas for Developing Skills

Level 4: Integrate Knowledge and Procedures
Execute plans, Solve problems

Current examples of conflicting codes. Have students choose a current problem in the US or another country in which codes conflict (e.g., sweatshops that employ children). Ask students to define what the conflicting codes are, describe what the purpose may have been for the codes, whether the purpose was good, explain different ways the conflict of codes could be resolved, and evaluate which resolution of conflicting codes is best and why. In conjunction with other skills or with community organizers, have students take action on their ideas about resolving a code conflict.

Assessment Hints

Judging code validity

Give students a wide range of problems from multiple contexts (e.g., school, family, political, environmental) and ask them to describe the appropriate set of codes for each context, explain why the codes are important, and determine the purpose of the code.

Present a set of codes to students and have them identify which situations are appropriate for each.

Present a description of a set of codes and how the codes might have come to be. Ask students to evaluate means by which the codes were created and the appropriateness (or "goodness") of the codes themselves.

Create a Climate
to Develop Using Codes

- Encourage students' commitment to making the best decisions for family, schools, neighborhood, and community. Have students refer to their commitments periodically for assignments.

- Encourage students' commitment to be a good citizen within school, family, community, state, country, and world (e.g., respecting and having concern for others, being of service to their community, taking personal responsibility for their actions and intentions).

- Promote students' feeling and taking responsibility/accountability for their actions through disciplining students with immediate consequences and a given reason and helping parents with discipline plans that include giving reasons to students when disciplined.

- Emphasize the importance of feeling connected to others. Establish classroom community by encouraging students to collaborate on assignments and projects. Encourage respectful interactions among students in class, and encourage students to connect with other students outside the classroom (or their "group" or "clique") and members in their community.

- Encourage students' commitment to justice/fairness. Discuss students' experiences of injustice. Read about leaders for social justice. Perform a social justice action in the community.

Sample Student Self-Monitoring
Using Codes

Encourage active learning by having students learn to monitor their own learning

Characterizing codes

Do I know how to identify what codes, rules, and laws apply to this problem?

Do I know how to apply the codes to this particular situation?

What are the unspoken codes in this situation?

Discerning code application

Do I know how to find out what the codes are in this situation?

Did I identify all of the appropriate rules that apply to this problem?

Did I identify all of the appropriate laws that apply to this problem?

Judging code validity

Do I know how to evaluate whether the codes in this situation are appropriate or good?

What codes, rules, or laws would my parents/teacher/principal/neighbor/friend use in solving this problem?

Understanding Consequences

(Know consequences)

WHAT

Understanding consequences involves understanding the relationships between events and their consequences and then using that understanding to predict the possible consequences of actions being considered. It is important to be able to think about both short-term and long-term consequences, as well considering all the people who may be affected by an action. We need to be prepared for unforeseen consequences. We must practice and refine creative responses.

WHY

Most people, but especially teenagers, do not automatically consider consequences when they are dealing with a situation. Further, we tend to ignore possible negative consequences and only pay attention to the potential outcomes that are positive. Part of learning from the past is the practice of identifying consequences of past actions in order to become better at predicting consequences of potential options. It is important to practice responses rather than learn during or after an event. Responding to negative events is a difficult endeavor that we learn from experience.

Web Wise

The United Nations Human Rights Commission has teaching tools on refugees: www.unhcr.ch

Anti-Defamation League: http://www.adl.org/awod/awod_institute.html

http://www.ideafinder.com/home.htm

SUBSKILLS OVERVIEW

1: Attending to consequences

Looking at the past and connecting consequences with their causes

Understanding that big consequences can result from small actions

Understanding the importance of considering consequences outside one's immediate concern

2: Predicting consequences

Short-term & long-term consequences

Positive & negative consequences

3: Responding to consequences

Chapter books about consequences:
Armstrong, W. (1989). *Sounder*. New York: Harper & Row.
Fox, P. (1984). *One-eyed cat*. Scarsdale, NY: Bradbury.
Myers, W. (1988). *Scorpions*. New York: Harper Collins.
Myers, W. (1992). *Somewhere in the darkness*. New York: Scholastic.
Naylor, P. (1991). *Shiloh*. New York: Athenum.

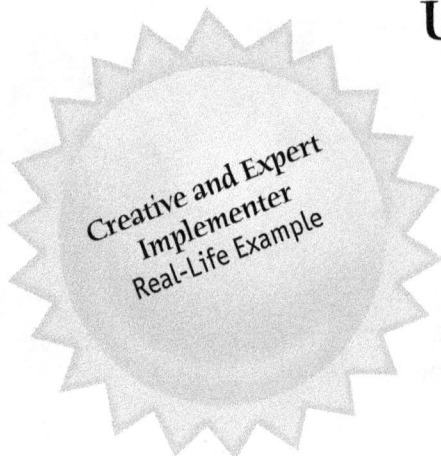

Understanding Consequences by Attending to Them

Creative and Expert Implementer Real-Life Example

Economists in the U.S. have become more and more sensitive to just how much global events impact the U.S. economy. The consequences of civil disruption in the Middle East or a major election in Asia will more than likely show up in some manner in the complex and sensitive American economy.

Ideas for Developing Skills

Level 1: Immersion in Examples and Opportunities
Attend to the big picture, Learn to recognize basic patterns

Consequences in history. (1) Have students compare and contrast the consequences of lying or telling the truth in times of revolution or war. (2) Identify a famous person in history and have students identify what consequences they cared about (e.g., poverty). What causes of those consequences did they want to change (e.g., unfair working wages)? (3) Look at a particular institution or practice today (as a consequence) and examine what happened historically to cause or influence it.

Stories of consequences in social institutions. Read stories or historical accounts that depict causes and consequences in terms of the creation of hospitals, schools, police.

Stories of consequences in scientific discovery. Read stories or historical accounts that depict causes and consequences in terms of how science has advanced. Causes can include politics, ambition, curiosity, while consequences can include technological advance, human oppression, saving the earth, human health, etc.

Stories of consequences in art and music. Read stories or historical accounts that depict causes and consequences in terms of how art and music are related to the time period and cultures in which they were created (as well as how they relate to how they're expressed today, i.e., song connected to a patriotic incident).

Stories of consequences in business. Read stories or historical accounts that depict causes and consequences in terms of how businesses market their products and how consumers respond.

Understanding Consequences by Attending to Them
Ideas for Developing Skills

Level 2: Attention to Facts and Skills
Focus on detail and prototypical knowledge, Build knowledge

Analyzing the consequences of one's everyday choices. To develop practical consciousness and develop constructive responses, students can start with easy decisions, like whether to eat junk food or nutritional food, asking questions such as, "Who benefits when I eat this hamburger?" Where do all the ingredients of this hamburger come from (e.g., pickles from Pennsylvania, buns from Ohio, beef from Central America, etc.)? What resources of the earth are being used in the creation of the hamburger (e.g., beef cattle are being raised on land razed from rainforest)? Is this the best use of the resources? How do my choices (e.g., clothes purchases, transportation) affect the well being of my community? How do my choices affect the global health of the planet?

Relational consequences. (1) Have students make a map of who they are related to and which of their own behaviors might affect those people. (2) Have students map members of their family of previous generations who have passed away and identify choices the ancestors made that affect the student today. (3) Read stories about consequences endured or enjoyed by a later generation in a particular family or community resulting from an ancestor's choices.

Media depiction of consequences. Have students watch and read advertisements for products that interest them and identify what consequences the advertiser implies will happen if you do or don't have the product. Are these consequences true to life?

My identity. Ask students to consider their goals for themselves and who they want to be. Have them reflect on what consequences would hinder reaching their goals and what resources they could use to overcome the obstacles.

Hearing victims' stories. Use written material or classroom visits if possible for students to hear how victims are affected by bad decisions (drunk driving, violence, etc.).

Level 3: Practice Procedures
Set goals, Plan steps of problem solving, Practice skills

Discussing risks with a mentor. Match students with older mentors to explore consequences of actions for risky behavior (such as drinking and driving). This could be done on an individual basis or by matching classrooms (i.e., the older class plans and performs a skit for the younger class). Older students will need some training in how to present their ideas clearly and responsibly.

Understanding Consequences by Attending to Them
Ideas for Developing Skills

Level 3 (continued)

Consequences of being a role model. (1) Have students select a role model. How do the choices that role model makes affect them, their perceptions of the world, and their goals for life? (2) Have students identify a younger child who likes them. Ask them to reflect on how their own choices affect that child, his or her perceptions of the world, and his or her goals for life?

Effects of our actions. Set up classroom rules and decision-making processes democratically so students gain experience in affecting their environment. Emphasize that big acts, like voting, matter, as do small acts, such as picking up a piece of trash.

Local community stakeholders. Have students interview community members. Students can write a report that addresses these issues: Who are the stake holders in my community? How are they affected by others' actions? Why should I care? How does this affect me? What can I do to help create positive consequences and change?

Level 4: Integrate Knowledge and Procedures
Execute plans, Solve problems

Be a mentor. Have students practice mentoring younger kids (see Appendix for guidance on cross-age tutoring).

Journaling on consequences. Have students journal on the choices they make through the day. Then have them analyze the consequences of their actions—from immediate consequences to long-term consequences, from effects on people around them and on people far away or in future generations, from personal consequences to consequences on the planet. Discuss how they can make a positive difference if they change one behavior. Have students select a behavior to change and practice it for a few weeks. They should journal on their progress (e.g., How hard is it to change this choice? Am I making a better choice?). After they have success with one, they should make another change. Discuss the outcomes in class.

Assessment Hints

Relating events to consequences

Link actions with consequences. Alone or within a group, students chart the relation between characters' choices and actions with the consequences for a particular dilemma.

Journal on relationships between actions and consequences. Use any hypothetical situation (video, story) to reflect on how consequences were tied to actions of the characters.

Individual performance. Following a cooperative or class activity targeting a particular judgment skill, students are assessed on their individual performance using a new example.

Understanding Consequences by Predicting Them

A **SWAT team captain** trying to handle a hostage situation has to be an expert at considering every possible consequence to every aspect of the situation.

Ideas for Developing Skills

Level 1: Immersion in Examples and Opportunities
Attend to the big picture, Learn to recognize basic patterns

Consequences in the media. Have students watch media in which consequences are or are not realistic (e.g., wrestling). Have them consider what would be realistic consequences.

Consequences of courtesy. Have students find examples of the ways courtesy and discourtesy of others affects them and vice versa.

Identifying consequences. Present the students with several behaviors (such as smoking, drinking and driving, etc.) and ask them to identify several possible consequences, including short-term & long-term, positive & negative, personal and non-personal (some contexts to think about are relationships, resources, community, etc).

Trigger phrases. Individually or as a group, have students develop phrases to trigger reflection on consequences (e.g., "Is this something I would be proud of?").

Level 2: Attention to Facts and Skills
Focus on detail and prototypical knowledge, Build knowledge

Patterns of consequences. Make a list of risky behaviors (such as using drugs, sex, gang membership, cheating, stealing, etc.) and a list of possible consequences (including consequences that can result from more than one behavior). Ask the students to draw lines between the matching behaviors and consequences and have them discuss the common consequences in particular (such as poor grades, limited future, costs lots of money). See Begun, 1996, *Ready-to-use Social Skills Lessons & Activities* for worksheets. Assess understanding with their responses to a new list.

Starred ★ activities within each subskill go together!

Understanding Consequences by Predicting Them
Ideas for Developing Skills

Level 2 (continued)

Personal choices. Think of behaviors that students make choices about (e.g., what to spend money on, sex, drinking, drugs, stealing, fights). (1) Have the students list out possible consequences (positive and negative) for their choices and mark the consequences that matter to them. Discuss and re-do the list afterwards (to add new ideas from the discussion). (2) Have students interview older students about what they think the consequences are for those same choices and which ones matter to them. Combine this list with the previous list. (3) Have students interview elders in the community about the possible consequences for those same choices and which ones matter to them. Combine this list with the previous lists. Map or graph all consequences as a class.

Consequences of moderation. (1) Identify areas in which too little or too much has negative consequences: eating, shopping, partying, exercising, talking on the phone, surfing the web, etc. Have them identify ways to help themselves maintain moderation. (2) Have students identify areas where only a little rather than a lot has better consequences for others: e.g., making garbage, hitting someone on the shoulder as a friendly greeting, etc.

Group decision making. Have students practice making decisions in groups so that they have to consider the multiple consequences that different people generate. Make sure they get many people's input on whether specific consequences are important or not (rather than single-person vetoes). Ask them to reflect on this process.

How much does a baby cost? Make up a worksheet with some common baby items such as food, diapers, a visit to the pediatrician, etc. Ask students to estimate the cost of each of these items and then have them research the actual cost in a store or on the internet. This activity could also be used to reflect on costs of drug use, smoking, and other health problems. See Begun, 1996, *Ready-to-use Social Skills Lessons & Activities* for worksheets.

Level 3: Practice Procedures
Set goals, Plan steps of problem solving, Practice skills

Starred ★ activities within each subskill go together!

★ **Resource use as a citizen of the world.** Have students discuss and write about the consequences of natural resource alternatives. What resources are abundant? Which are scarce? What conflicts are there over resources? How are resources conserved? How are they wasted? What are the consequences of wasted resources? What are examples of wasted resources from our own history? What are ways to conserve what we have? Students can consult the book, *50 Ways To Save The Planet*.

Understanding Consequences by Predicting Them
Ideas for Developing Skills

Level 3 (continued)

Weighing positive and negative consequences. Select a decision that can have positive consequences in some situations and negative consequence in other situations (such as telling the truth when it is the right thing to do versus when it could hurt someone) and ask students to list the consequences of telling the truth in both situations.

Considering consequences from different perspectives. Select an ethical dilemma that involves several people and ask students to generate possible consequences for each of the people involved.

Level 4: Integrate Knowledge and Procedures
Execute plans, Solve problems

Considering direct and indirect consequences. Select an ethical dilemma involving both personal impact on those involved as well as community/global impact and ask students to consider both direct and indirect consequences.

Global effects of my habits. Have students select one of their pastimes or habits and explore its consequences on others. They will have to find out the origin of any materials that are used and the process of making any human-made aspect of the activity including its cost on the humans finding or making it. For example, for the activity of eating bananas, one must find out the pathway of the bananas from their origin to the mouth of the consumer. Who grew them and what consequence did it have on that person and their community? Who shipped them to the U.S. and etc.? Who moved them from the port to the local store and etc.? Who sells them, etc.?

Assessment Hints

Predicting consequences

Generate possible consequences. Students generate possible consequences alone or within a group for a particular dilemma.

Stopping a video or story. Stopping a video or story at a critical moment, ask students to identify possible consequences.

Individual performance. Following a cooperative or class activity targeting a particular judgment skill, students are assessed on their individual performance using a new example.

Starred ★ activities within each subskill go together!

EJ-5 Understanding Consequences

Understanding Consequences by Responding to Them

Erin Brockovich responded to consequences and helped an entire community. She helped to identify the cause of a community's physical ailments: polluted drinking water. She then responded to this by convincing attorneys to sue the company who knowingly polluted the water and lied to the community about it. In the end, the lawsuit was settled for a record amount, $333 million.

After seven people died from cyanide placed in Tylenol in 1962, **Johnson and Johnson** spent $200 million to make tamper-proof containers. After this, pharmaceutical companies moved to using tamper-proof containers, helping everyone using over-the-counter medications to be safer.

Ideas for Developing Skills

Level 1: Immersion in Examples and Opportunities
Attend to the big picture, Learn to recognize basic patterns

Responding to environmental consequences. (1) Business practices (e.g., dumping hazardous waste): for example, investigate local community history to find out what businesses have done in response to finding out that they have caused harm to persons or the environment. (2) Civic design (freeways, increased commuting, landfills, no recycling): for example, investigate local community: what is the community doing to alleviate, for example, the harm done by poor planning and poor refuse disposal?

Careers that respond to consequences. Watch films about or bring in guest speakers who are first responders (e.g., fire fighters, police officers, hospital emergency room personnel). Discuss what actions brought about particular consequences and what the personnel had to do to minimize the damage.

How people respond to negative consequences they caused. (1) Find examples in which persons do not take responsibility for the damage they have caused. Instead they deny responsibility or blame someone or something else. (2) Find examples of people taking responsibility and making amends for the harm they have caused.

Starred ★ activities within each subskill go together!

Short-term vs. long-term consequences. Often people make decisions based on short-term consequences. Frequently, it is hard to foresee long-term consequences. Sometimes we just have to sit down and think about it. Have students identify the short- and long-term consequences of particular actions.

Understanding Consequences
by Responding to Them
Ideas for Developing Skills

Level 1 (continued)

What if the negative consequences are to you? Have students inter-view community members about personal suffering from other people's actions. Interviewees should describe the situation and how they explain it and how they responded. Students report to class.

Examples of learning from negative consequences. Present and discuss examples of situations where a person did not use or have good character skills and suffered the consequences (the person and the com-munity). For example, (a) a person who lied, (b) a person who reacted impulsively, (c) a person who was prejudiced,   (d) a person who made war instead of peace, (e) a person who did not did not work hard, (f) a person who did not respect a tradition, (g) a person who did not take up leadership to work for the welfare of others, (h) a person who was not assertive and did not speak up for others, (i) a person who was unable to resolve things without violence.

Level 2: Attention to Facts and Skills
Focus on detail and prototypical knowledge, Build knowledge

How do I know if the situation turned out the right way? We evaluate the consequences of our actions according to how we perceive our obligations (see a suggested list below). Discuss stories of characters whose actions create consequences for others. Students decide which obligations they honored and which ones were ignored. Here is a list of obligations from Sir W. David Ross (1939):
- Keeping one's word
- Making amends
- Showing gratitude
- Fairness
- Improving the lives of others
- Not hurting others
- Self improvement in character
- Self improvement in intelligence

Responding to "relational consequences". Use the maps generated by the "relational consequences" activity in the Attending to Consequences subskill (p. 107). Have each student: (a) Select a behavior of theirs that had consequences for others and describe what the behavior was and what the consequences were; have students discuss what the student could do about the negative consequences they caused. (b) Select a behavior of an ancestor or elder that had consequences for the student, and describe what it was and what the consequences were; have students discuss what the student can do to overcome negative consequences that affect them.

EJ-5 Understanding Consequences

Starred ★ activities
within each subskill
go together!

Understanding Consequences by Responding to Them
Ideas for Developing Skills

Level 2 (continued)

Historical responses to negative consequences. Discuss what was done to respond to negative consequences in particular historical situations. What caused the harm? Who was responsible? What did the responsible party do to alleviate the harm? What might have happened if they had not tried to alleviate the harm? What else might have been done additionally or instead? For example: (a) post-war reparations (e.g., the Marshall plan was instituted to rebuild Germany after many cities were bombed out during the Second World War), (b) slavery in the United States.

Responses to negative consequences of criminal behavior. Discuss how society should respond to (a) someone who drives while intoxicated, (b) someone who robs to get money to purchase drugs for an addiction, (c) someone who shoplifts something they want.

Responses to negative consequences in business world. Students gather information about specific incidents in the business world in which the public or innocent parties suffered much harm. The students should identify what the harmful practice was and what harm it did. Suggestions of scandals to study include: Enron, Arthur Anderson, and WorldCom.

Responses to positive consequences. Sometimes people do not respond well to sudden or great positive consequences such as winning the lottery or celebrity. Have students find examples of those who responded well and those who did not. Compare the characteristics and behaviors of each group.

How family members respond to relational consequences. Students identify negative consequences in relationships and find out whether or not their family members have experienced them and how they responded.

What if bad things happen to you? Brainstorm a list of negative things that can happen to you. Then brainstorm ways to respond to each one in terms of how you explain it and in terms of what you do about it. Role play appropriate responses to negative events.

How to learn from negative consequences. Read cases or stories where a person made a mistake in judgment, sensitivity, or other area of character skills. Have students discuss what the person learned from their mistake or what they should have learned.

Starred ★ activities within each subskill go together!

Understanding Consequences by Responding to Them
Ideas for Developing Skills

Level 3: Practice Procedures
Set goals, Plan steps of problem solving, Practice skills

Responses to negative consequences of a hurtful relationship. (1) Discuss what kinds of behaviors are not acceptable in intimate relationships. Then do one or more of the following. (a) Watch a movie or read a story about a person who helps someone escape abuse. Discuss what a person (what the students) should do if a family member or friend is being psychologically, physically or sexually abused. (b) Discuss what a person should do if they are being abused. Website references for this information include www.coalitionagainstabuse.com and www.fvpf.org. (2) Discuss what kinds of behaviors are bullying behaviors. Read a story or watch a film about bullying. Discuss what a person should do to intervene when bullying occurs. Discuss what to do when someone bullies you. Discuss what to do instead when you feel angry and want to bully someone.

Alternative responses to crime. (1) Have students gather information about alternative responses (and compare with traditional responses) to crime such as restorative justice, peace circles, and community courts. Have students write an essay about the advantages and disadvantages. (2) Bring in guest speakers to discuss alternative responses to crime such as restorative justice, peace circles, and community courts. Ask them to point out the advantages and disadvantages of the approach. Have students write a response to the speaker with follow up questions. (3) Have students observe and report on an alternative process in the local community.

Responding to relational consequences. Students make a map that indicates who they are related to. This should include their immediate family (or guardians), extended family and immediate ancestors. The student indicates what choices these people have made that have consequences for the student. Teacher should write each consequence on a piece of paper, separately and anonymously. Include all consequences students have identified and add some additional feasible consequences. Put all pieces of paper in a hat and pull one out to discuss: How can the student respond to the consequence? What choices does the student have? How can the student overcome the negatives? How can the student take advantage of the positives? (The teacher may have to prepare ahead with ideas.)

Journal on learning from negative consequences. Look at the full list of character skills (from these materials or a combination of materials) that the class or school is working on. Have students keep track of their lack of skills on one or a subset of the skills. Each day they should reflect on how they used the skill, how well they used the skill, and what the consequences were.

EJ-5 Understanding Consequences

Starred ★ activities within each subskill go together!

Understanding Consequences by Responding to Them
Ideas for Developing Skills

Level 4: Integrate Knowledge and Procedures
Execute plans, Solve problems

What if you caused the negative consequences for others?
(a) Students identify a negative consequence they have caused and create a plan for taking responsibility and making amends. Have students follow through and then report on what happened. (b) Students keep a journal for a week or more and keep track of the negative consequences they caused and how they made up for it. Coach students so that they improve over the period of the project.

Dealing with consequences in the community. Have students identify a problem in the community that is the consequence of the activities of prior residents or businesses (e.g., hazardous waste or trash, vandalized bus stop). Use the steps suggested by Lewis et al. (1998) in *Kid's Guide to Social Action* (written for kids to use with worksheets and concrete guidelines): (1) Choose a problem in the neighborhood (Does an area feel unsafe? Smell bad? Look terrible? Are there needy people?). (2) Do your research (How do community members feel about the problem? What is the history of the problem?). (3) Brainstorm possible solutions and choose the one that seems most possible and will make the most difference. (4) Build coalitions of support. Find all the people that agree with you (neighborhood, community, city, state, businesses, agencies). (5) Figure out (with the help of your coalition) who is your opposition and work with them on overcoming their objections. (6) Advertise (send out a news release, call tv, radio, newspaper reporters, churches). (7) Raise money if you need to. (8) Carry out your solution. Make a list of the steps you need to take (e.g., write letters, give speeches, pass petitions). (9) Evaluate and reflect on whether the plan is working. Did you try everything, should you change something? Celebrate what you have done by writing about it, dramatizing it, drawing it. (10) Don't give up. Find the thing that will work.

Assessment Hints

Responding to consequences

Journal. Students write about the positive and negative consequences they cause over a period of time (e.g., one week).

Story completion. Finish stories with consequences and outcomes.

Role play. Have students role play how they should respond to consequences in various challenging situations.

Reflective activities. Have students write esssays or keep a journal about how they respond to consequences.

Social action projects. Have students show how they should respond to consequences of social issues. Projects include petitions, demonstrations, letter writing, advocacy, and campaigning.

Create a Climate
to Develop Skills in Understanding Consequences

Reflection periods
- Provide time for students to consider the consequences of decisions they make.
- Give the students opportunities to return to problems they worked on to reflect on the outcomes (particularly the long term consequences).
- Encourage the taking of responsibility of actions that cause harm. Do so without ridicule or scorn, but as a matter of learning, growth and self-improvement.

Promoting participation in the group decision making
- Allow for student decision making within limits.
- Use your power, by virtue of your role, only when necessary.
- Emphasize the class group identity in a positive way.
- Provide opportunities for cooperative behavior as a large group.
- Illustrate the negative effects of not working together as a large group.
- Emphasize the positive impact the group can have on others.

Sample Student Self-Monitoring
Understanding Consequences

Encourage active learning by having students learn to monitor their own learning

Attending to consequences

I understand the difference between long-term and short-term effects.

I understand that any time a decision is made, there are almost always both long-term and short-term consequences.

Predicting consequences

What situations are familiar to me from the past that resemble this situation?

What were the outcomes?

What is different about this situation?

What could be done?

How can I get help figuring this out?

What might happen?

How can I verify what might happen?

Responding to consequences

I pay attention to the effects I have on others.

I try not to cause harmful effects to others.

I make amends when I have done something to cause harmful effects to others.

I know how to not blame others for things I am responsible for.

I avoid denying what I have caused.

Reflecting on the Process and Outcome

(Think back)

WHAT

Reflection is an important metacognitive (or thinking about thinking) skill. It consists of examining one's thinking processes and outcomes. For students to consistently make good ethical decisions, they must reflect on both their *judgment process* and their *resulting decision*. Making right choices is complicated. To hone our choices into right choices, we must reflect on all that we do and orient our minds to do the right thing.

WHY

Being able to reflect on thinking processes and outcomes is related to growth in social understanding, ethical behavior, and expertise. Reflection is one thing that distinguishes humans from animals. Animals are ruled by instincts, whereas with reflection and self-awareness, humans can change their instinctive behaviors when they are harmful. It is easy to do the wrong thing. The wrong thing is an action that ends up hurting someone else. So if we make an off-the-cuff critical remark, it may end up hurting someone. If we are unaware of our thoughtlessness, we can cause pain. Reflection and focusing on the right help us avoid doing harm.

SUBSKILLS OVERVIEW

1: Reasoning about means and ends
> Assessing viability of options
> Determining appropriateness of actions
> Assessing effects of actions

2: Making right choices

3: Monitoring one's reasoning
> Monitoring the reasoning processes before, during, after
> Monitoring the products of reasoning

Sir W. David Ross, a well-known philosopher who wrote *Foundations of Ethics* (1939) lists the types of duties or obligatory actions that humans have:
- Keeping one's word
- Making amends
- Showing gratitude
- Fairness
- Improving the lives of others
- Not hurting others
- Self improvement in character
- Self improvement in intelligence

Web Wise

Find ideas and lesson plans at http://www.sciencenetlinks.com or http://www.marcopolosearch.org

Reflecting on the Process & Outcomes by Reasoning about the Means and Ends

Creative and Expert Implementer Real-Life Example

Politicians try to solve social problems with legislation. They often disagree on what means are appropriate to reach particular ends. For example, does increasing the minimum wage decrease poverty? Does gun ownership decrease crime?

Ideas for Developing Skills

Level 1: Immersion in Examples and Opportunities
Attend to the big picture, Learn to recognize basic patterns

What means should be used? Present examples from several domains in which a person or an expert must decide on what means to use to reach a particular end (e.g., for less crime: more police, crackdown on minor misdemeanors, curfews; for money for college: spend less and save more, have a budget, work another job, go to a less expensive college).

What ends or goals are worthwhile? Present examples from several domains in which a person or an expert tries to decide on what ends or goals to aim for (e.g., should I save money for college, a car, or adventure traveling).

Level 2: Attention to Facts and Skills
Focus on detail and prototypical knowledge, Build knowledge

Reflecting on poor decisions. Present to students both hypothetical and real-life examples of decision-making situations in which a poor decision was made. Assist them in assessing the poor decision. Have them evaluate each of the following: the viability of the options, the effects of the decision on others and self, and the overall appropriateness of the decision. Ask them to determine why the decision was poor, based on their evaluation of the three criteria. Have students make a new decision and go through the three criteria again to ensure that it's a good decision.

Steps for reflection? Means and ends. Reflection involves monitoring your reasoning process and assessing the decision you made. Focus students' attention to what assessing their decision looks like. Present to students examples of decision-making situations (e.g., you see your friend cheating on a test). Assist the students through the reasoning process by cueing them to think about options, what each option represents (honesty, loyalty, etc.), and reasons behind the options. Help them to collectively make a decision. Then review with them the viability of the options, the effects of the decision on others and self, and the overall appropriateness of the decision. After the review, point out to students that they were assessing the adequacy of the decision.

Starred ★ activities within each subskill go together!

Reflecting on the Process & Outcomes by Reasoning about the Means and Ends
Ideas for Developing Skills

Level 2 (continued)

Exploring means and ends in a fictional character's judgment processes. Give students ethical dilemmas in which the character makes a decision and the character's judgment process and decision are described (e.g., in literature, court case, movies). Ask students to describe the judgment process that the character used and to evaluate whether the character's decision was appropriate. Questions for the students to answer include the following. What options did the character consider? Were there other options that the character did not consider? What consequences did he or she think about in making this decision? What codes, standards, or ideals did the character consider? What was the deciding factor of the character's decision? Do you think the character's decision was appropriate? Why or why not?

Level 3: Practice Procedures
Set goals, Plan steps of problem solving, Practice skills

Evaluating judgment process and outcome. Present students with an ★ ethical dilemma in which they make a decision about what to do (use real-life decision-making situations in your school and community). Afterwards, students reflect on their decision, evaluating the viability of the options, the effects of the decision on others and self, and the overall appropriateness of the decision. Ask them to state whether the judgment made was the most ethical and why.

Level 4: Integrate Knowledge and Procedures
Execute plans, Solve problems

Mentoring others in decision making. Assign students a younger student who needs assistance in an area of reasoning. Prepare the older students carefully to ensure that they consistently help the younger student reflect on whether the decision was good. Use real-life, curriculum-based, or simple decision situations. ★

Starred ★ activities
within each subskill
go together!

Assessment Hints

Reasoning about means and ends

Use multiple-choice, true-false, short answer, or essay tests to assess students' knowledge of reasoning about means and ends skills (e.g., assessing the viability of the options, the effects of the decision on others and self, the overall appropriateness of the decision).

Use a new ethical dilemma (with the character's judgment process described) and have students evaluate, or reflect on, the means and ends of the character's judgment process.

Reflecting on the Outcome by Making Right Choices

Creative and Expert Implementer Real-Life Example

Hugh Thompson was a helicopter pilot who risked his life to intervene and stop the massacre of innocent Vietnamese civilians at My Lai. The leader of the slaughter was Lieutenant Calley. Hugh Thompson and his crew were able to save 10 unarmed civilians, including a 5-year-old and prevented further slaughter beyond the 500 civilians who were killed. His biography is described in the book, *The Forgotten Hero of My Lai: The Hugh Thompson Story* by Trent Angers (1999).

Ideas for Developing Skills

Level 1: Immersion in Examples and Opportunities
Attend to the big picture, Learn to recognize basic patterns

What tempts you away from your duties? Often a person doesn't do his or her duty because of pleasurable distractions, because they don't want to make the effort, or because they are insensitive to the situation (usually because they have something else on their mind like pleasure). Read stories or watch a video that shows a character tempted away from their duties. Discuss what the temptation was, and what the character might have done to counteract it.

Right choice making in action. Invite an expert to speak about how they make morally good choices in their work. Have them point out the challenges to making moral decisions and what happens when immoral decisions are made. Ask them to solve a problem out loud.

Level 2: Attention to Facts and Skills
Focus on detail and prototypical knowledge, Build knowledge

What are our duties? Discuss Ross' chart of duties. Ask students to discuss several decision situations and how to resolve them in accordance with one's obligations.

What makes a choice right? Present a story or video in which a character makes a decision. Discuss with the students whether the decision and action were right. An action is right if it produces more good than any other act. Discuss what other choices there were and which was the right (most moral—producing the most good) choice.

Starred ★ activities within each subskill go together!

Reflecting on the Outcome by Making Right Choices
Ideas for Developing Skills

Level 2 (continued)

How people think about the right choice as "fitting"—by domain.
Select a domain and discuss 'right' and 'wrong' choices within the domain in the sense of what fits philosophically/historically with the focus of the domain and in the sense of what is morally right. Invite experts to lead the discussion. Provided on the right are some examples of domains and what might be right in practice (fit choices) and what might be morally right.

What are right choices? In order to determine what boundaries there are on your choices, you need to consider where you are in life, what your responsibilities are and what your goals are. Discuss one or more of the topics below in relation to the duties that Ross lists (see chart). What do the duties themselves look like in this area? What are the challenges? What skills help you make right choices? What resources help you make right choices? (a) What are right choices at my age? (b) What are right choices as a boy or girl? (c) What are right choices for my future? (d) What are right choices for my body? (e) What are right choices for supporting my family? (f) What are right choices for supporting my community? (g) What are right choices for supporting my school? (h) What are right choices for supporting my city/state/country?

How to tell if you've made the right choice. Discuss how people know they've made the right choice (approval from others who want the best for you, feeling good inside, community approval, rewards). After discussing the choices within the different areas above, discuss actual situations (student or teacher generated, historical or literary). Were duties as a human being followed? Was more good brought about than harm? Did the choice make the person feel good inside?

When in doubt, don't. Some people make decisions based on the maxim: When in doubt, don't (do it). So that when you are uncertain or are wavering about a choice, it is better not to do it. (Much of the time when you make a choice you are uncertain about, you regret it later. Part of choosing not to do it is letting it go and believing that something better will come along.) Have students bring up issues of concern to themselves personally and as a group. Discuss the benefits of not choosing an action in the particular circumstances.

Making amends when you made the wrong choice. How to apologize: express regret (must be real) for your actions and concern for the other person's feelings. Don't minimize the harm you have caused. How not to apologize (from P. M. Forni, 2002, *Choosing Civility*): "I'm sorry but I am under a lot of stress" (this is excusing yourself), apologizing after making people wait in a grocery line as you run back to get something in the middle of checking out (this is a self-authorization to be inconsiderate). Have students practice apologizing and keeping track of what happened and what they said.

Domain examples with fit and right choices:

SCIENCE: Fit choices in science would involve using data, empirical evidence, testable and falsifiable hypotheses. Inappropriate choices would involve relying on personal perceptions and feelings, anecdotes, and so on. Issues of moral rightness/wrongness would include: cloning, deception in experiments with humans, use of animals in experiments.

WRITING: Fit choices in writing would involve avoiding clichés, using correct grammar, vocabulary and structure, and so on. Moral rightness/wrongness issues in writing would include copying someone else's work and claiming it as your own (recent examples of this are the historians Doris Kearns Goodwin and Stephen Ambrose), perpetuating lies or conveying false information (as David Brooks recently admitted doing in his books about Anita Hill and Hilary Clinton).

BUSINESS: Fit choices in business would involve whatever benefits most either the shareholders (usual these days) or the stakeholders (workers, customers, shareholders). Moral rightness would includes issues of effects of business operations in local communities (e.g., health, environment), issues of product quality and fidelity.

CIVIC DOMAIN: Fit choices in civic institutions would involve practices that support constituents. Moral rightness issues include effects on non-constituents, effects on future generations, and hidden environmental effects.

Starred ⭐ activities within each subskill go together!

EJ-6 Reflecting on the Process and Outcome

Reflecting on the Outcome
by Making Right Choices
Ideas for Developing Skills

Level 3: Practice Procedures
Set goals, Plan steps of problem solving, Practice skills

What can lead you to make the wrong choice? Find examples in real life, literature, or film of people who made the wrong choice. Analyze what drove them to do so. Discuss how to avoid making bad choices (e.g., stand up against pressure; control your fear of reproach; control your fear of the person involved; be open to the unfamiliar rather than choosing what is comfortable and familiar; don't repeat unhealthy or false messages in your head like "I'm taking their property because I need it more than they do" or "They deserve to be punished." Have students analyze a historical or literary situation for the reasons behind the choices made. Have them write an alternative ending that involves making good choices.

Level 4: Integrate Knowledge and Procedures
Execute plans, Solve problems

Government decision making. (1) Have students observe the local government in action (e.g., city council meeting). Have them take notes on what was discussed and decided. Bring the information back to class and discuss whether or not the right choices were made. Students should defend their positions using solid reasoning, concern for their obligations, and sensitivity to local context. (2) Select a local issue (e.g., taxes, pollution, waste management) and have the students take on the roles of government officials and role play a decision-making situation.

Addressing a school or community issue. Have students select an issue or problem in the school or community that people agree needs to be changed. Have students gather ideas from community members of various ages and backgrounds about how they think things should change.

Assessment Hints

Making right choices

Have students write an essay about a person who made wrong and then right choices.

Have students complete reflective activities (such as essays, keeping a report diary) about making right choices.

Have students keep a journal about making right choices. Journal options include regular, dialogue journals (teacher writes back), literature response journals, simulated journals, and email journals.

Starred ★ activities
within each subskill
go together!

Reflecting on the Process & Outcome by Monitoring One's Reasoning

Supreme Court Justice, **Ruth Bader Ginsburg** is an expert in monitoring her reasoning. Justice Ginsburg is known for her scholarly, balanced opinions.

Creative and Expert Implementer Real-Life Example

Ideas for Developing Skills

Level 1: Immersion in Examples and Opportunities
Attend to the big picture, Learn to recognize basic patterns

What is reflection? Self-monitoring. Reflection involves monitoring your reasoning process and assessing the decision you made. Present examples of what monitoring reasoning looks like. Present to students examples of decision-making situations in which experts think aloud as they analyze and solve a problem.

Examples of monitoring reasoning. (1) Show excerpts from television shows, videos, or radio in which experts guide the viewer in accomplishing a task. Discuss how this step-by-step approach can be applied to monitoring reasoning. (2) Show a video excerpt from a teacher thinking aloud about a problem as he or she solves it for the class. (3) Ask students to videotape or audiotape adults solving a reasoning problem (in a particular subject or domain). Watch or listen to tapes in class and identify main features of problem solving using reasoning.

Emotions and reflection. Emotions can both be a guide to decision making and a hindrance. When stable, emotions can temper cold reason (e.g., city council evicting a non-profit food shelter because putting a parking ramp in that location would make money). However, when inflamed, emotions can derail good reasoning (e.g., community members screaming irrationally at city council members at a hearing about the food shelter eviction). Have students watch or read examples of both types of emotional influence and discuss. What outcomes result from these extreme emotional states? Does this mean that emotion should not play a role in reasoning and reflection? (No, just extreme emotion).

Level 2: Attention to Facts and Skills
Focus on detail and prototypical knowledge, Build knowledge

Reflection assistance. Assist the students through the reasoning process by cueing them to think about options, what each option represents (honesty, loyalty, etc.), and the reasons behind the options. Write the process on the board, and help them to collectively make a decision. Then review the process with the students, seeing if they should have discussed more issues, options, or reasons. After the review, point out to students that they were reflecting on their reasoning process.

Starred ★ activities within each subskill go together!

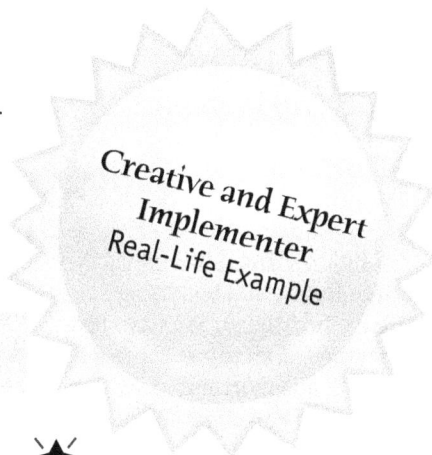

Reflecting on the Process & Outcome by Monitoring One's Reasoning
Ideas for Developing Skills

Level 2 (continued)

★ **Reflecting on the decision-making process.** In order for students to reflect on their reasoning process, they need to know what a typical reasoning process should look like. Present a decision-making algorithm to them, like the one below. Guide them through the process using examples (such as a community problem or decision to be made) and reflect on the process afterwards.
- Identify problem and decision to be made
- Consider all consequences (both positive and negative) of all alternatives, especially how alternative may affect others (including individuals in both the in- and out-group)
- Evaluate options (WHY and HOW about each alternative)
- Make a decision

Awareness of difficulty of different dilemmas. Students should understand that different dilemmas or decision-making situations make different demands on them. Give students a variety of ethical dilemmas with a large range of difficulty. Ask students to identify which ones are easy and which ones are difficult. Ask students to think about ethical dilemmas they encountered in the past and sort them according to difficulty. Lead a discussion to identify commonalities among the difficult versus the easy dilemmas.

The thinking strategy of summarizing. Present to students the various ethical dilemmas. Ask students to develop the various summaries or "cognitive maps" (i.e., visual representation) of the dilemmas. Summarize the critical information of the dilemma to help them remember the relevant information. As a small group discusses the dilemma, they record their thought process throughout the discussion (i.e., a description of the content and sequence of their decision-making process). Discuss with other students when and why using this strategy might be most helpful.

The thinking strategy of self-questioning. Present to students various ethical dilemmas. Ask students to use self-questioning to remember important information about the dilemmas and to review the thought process used to resolve the dilemma (i.e., the content and sequence of their decision-making process). Discuss with students when and why using this strategy might be most helpful.

Starred ★ activities
within each subskill
go together!

Sample ethical dilemmas
- You forgot that you had a science test today. You have not studied at all for it. You are offered an opportunity to cheat on it. Do you cheat?
- You are responsible for cleaning the house this afternoon. Your parents are having guests over for dinner this evening. A good friend stops by and wants you to go to a movie that you have been wanting to see. Do you go to the movie?
- As you were walking down the street, you saw a man reach into his pocket. As he pulled his hand out, a $20 bill came out and fell to the ground. The man didn't notice. Do you tell the man he dropped the money?
- Your friend tells you that he was the one who stole the teacher's wallet yesterday. He asks you not to tell anyone else. Do you promise him that you won't?
- You told your mom that you would watch your little sister so she can spend the afternoon with her friend who is in town for only one day. Now your friend is asking you to go to an autograph session of your favorite music group being held the same afternoon. What do you do?
- Your wealthy aunt visited your family last weekend. As she was leaving, she gave you a $100 check to spend however you would like. You could donate it to your class who is sponsoring a young boy in Paraguay, or you could buy a pocket videogame for yourself. What do you do?

Reflecting on the Process & Outcome
by Monitoring One's Reasoning
Ideas for Developing Skills

Level 3: Practice Procedures
Set goals, Plan steps of problem solving, Practice skills

Describing own judgment process. Present students with ethical dilemmas. Have them make a decision and write it down. Then ask the students to describe the judgment process that they used (e.g., thinking about specific options, consequences, codes, and reasons). Ask students to present the ethical dilemma to an adult (e.g., parent, family member) and have the adult think through the dilemma out loud, while the student records the thinking process. Finally, have them compare their judgment process to their interviewee's, and a comprehensive judgment process that the teacher presents in class (e.g., the process used in the Level 2 activity). Students evaluate their strengths and weaknesses in completing the judgment process.

Journaling about decision-making process. Have students keep a journal for a week or two. Ask them to write down at least one decision they made each day and whether they monitored their reasoning process during or after they made a decision. Ask them to evaluate how monitoring their reasoning (or not monitoring their reasoning) influenced the decision they made.

Ethical conflict/dilemmas discussion and self-monitoring. Students debate about ethical situations and decision-making (use community problems or issues if possible). After students debate, they describe how their thinking process should be improved in the future (e.g., take new factors into account, weigh certain consequences more heavily than others, etc.) when making decisions in the particular ethical situation discussed. Have students describe their ethical decision-making process before and after the debate. Ask the students to reflect on what they learned.

Starred ★ activities
within each subskill
go together!

Reflecting on the Process & Outcome
by Monitoring One's Reasoning
Ideas for Developing Skills

Level 4: Integrate Knowledge and Procedures
Execute plans, Solve problems

★ **Mentoring others in decision-making**. Assign students a younger student who needs assistance in an area of reasoning. Prepare the older students carefully to ensure that they are able to guide the younger student through a thorough decision-making process and ask concrete questions about whether everything was considered. Explain to the older students that the younger students probably do not have the reflection skills that they do, so they need to be very explicit and concrete in their reasoning guidance with the child. Use real-life, curriculum-based, or simple problems.

Assessment Hints

Monitoring one's reasoning

Present examples of reflection and non-reflection that vary in emotional intensity. Have students identify examples of good reflection with stable emotions. Also have students identify examples of poor reflection and explain why it is poor.

Use multiple-choice, true-false, short answer, or essay tests to assess students' knowledge of monitoring reasoning skills.

Use a new ethical dilemma (with the character's judgment process described) and have students evaluate (or reflect on) the reasoning process that the character used.

Starred ★ activities
within each subskill
go together!

Create a Climate
to Develop Using Codes

- Encourage students to think about their thinking of ethical issues. Encourage them to be conscious of their decision-making process.

- Encourage students to look at their decision-making process that they used after making an ethical decision.

- Encourage students to think about whether they made the right choice for family, school, neighborhood, and community after making an ethical decision.

- Encourage students to think about what the means and ends were in their decision after making an ethical decision. Were the "ends" of their decision the right choice? Were their "means" the most appropriate and ethical?

- Encourage students to reflect each day on their actions. Orient them to take actions that lead to good results for others. Ask them to make amends when they cause harm.

Sample Student Self-Monitoring
Developing Reflection Skills

Encourage active learning by having students learn to monitor their own learning

Monitoring one's reasoning

Did I define the problem accurately and entirely?

How difficult is this problem?

How much time did I spend making my decision?

Do I need to spend more time thinking about it?

Have my emotions affected my reasoning?

Did I think of all of the options?

If there are new options, how do they weigh against the other options considered?

Did I consider all of the consequences?

What is the probability of the consequences occurring?

Did I consider all of the codes, rules, or laws that apply to the problem?

What is the reason for my decision and why is it the best reason?

What is the product of my reasoning? Is it appropriate?

Making Right Choices

I know how to evaluate whether or not a right choice was made.

I try to make right choices.

I make amends when I make bad choices.

Reasoning about means and ends

How workable are the possible options that I thought of?

What are the effects of the decision on others?

What are the effects of the decision on myself?

How appropriate is the decision?

How appropriate are the consequences that result from the decision?

Coping
(Cope)

WHAT
Resiliency is a set of skills, behaviors and attitudes that allow a person beset by high risk factors to survive and to thrive in the face of adversity. Low coping skills leave one susceptible to risk behaviors like substance abuse, behavior problems and low achievement. Cognitive coping skills include thinking positively about others, having hope for a satisfying future, finding the silver lining in most experiences, and having positive perseverance under adverse conditions.

WHY
Research into the causes of poor life outcomes indicate that faulty thinking lies at the root of many contributing behaviors. Irrational beliefs inhibit healthy attitudes and behaviors. Positive thinking leads to improvements in health and achievement. What one believes makes a big difference in how your life unfolds.

SUBSKILLS OVERVIEW
1: Applying positive reasoning
- *Decatastrophizing* (thinking about both the best and worst case scenarios in adverse situations) vs. *catastrophizing* (thinking only about the worst case scenario)
- Identifying and countering negative thinking

2: Managing Disappointment and Failure

3: Developing resilience

Ten common irrational beliefs of children (Waters, 1982) that can lead to peer rejection, failure to achieve, behavior problems, substance abuse, and delinquent behavior.

1. Everything should go my way and I should always get what I want.
2. The world should be fair, and bad people should be punished.
3. Things should come easily for me.
4. I shouldn't show my feelings (I must be in complete control).
5. I shouldn't have to wait for anything.
6. I must win.
7. It's awful if other people don't like me.
8. There is only one right answer.
9. I'm bad if I make a mistake.
10. Adults should be perfect.

Web Wise
Find multiple lesson plans with assessments for building coping skills and resilience at www.projectresilience.com
http://www.ed.gov/databases/ERIC_Digests/ed386327.html
www.mentalhealth.org
Association for Applied and Therapeutic Humor: http://www.aath.org

---

ABC MODEL
(Seligman, 1995)

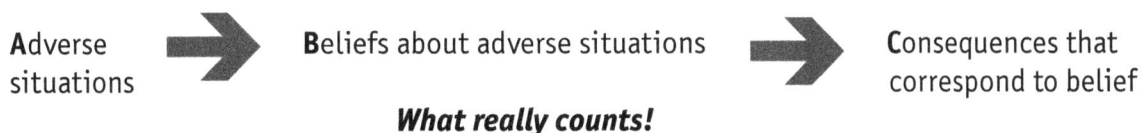

Adverse situations ➡ **B**eliefs about adverse situations ➡ **C**onsequences that correspond to belief

What really counts!

Coping
by Applying Positive Reasoning

Creative and Expert Implementer Real-Life Example

Abraham Lincoln did not engage in catastrophizing thinking during the Civil War. In other words, he did not limit his thinking to only the "worst case scenario" outcome for the war. Instead he remained an optimistic anti-slavery advocate and worked to achieve the best-case scenario outcome of the Civil War: a reunited United States.

Ideas for Developing Skills

Level 1: Immersion in Examples and Opportunities
Attend to the big picture, Learn to recognize basic patterns

Positive thinking in social situations. Discuss with students the importance of being positive when interacting with others. Role play positive and negative thinking with students. Describe a hypothetical social situation for students and role play a person with negative thinking (e.g., point to something wrong in everything with a pessimistic attitude) and ask students to interact with you. Then role play a person with positive thinking and have students interact with you. Facilitate a discussion among students about the differences between the two types of attitudes/thinking and which "character" students found more enjoyable and fun.

Positive thinking on the job. Invite experts to discuss how they use positive thinking in their work (you may have to search for people who do this consciously). For example, how do professionals who see troubled/ disturbed people most of the time (probation officers, social workers, counselors, police officers) maintain a positive outlook?

Alternative thoughts. Watch videos/films/television shows in which a character frequently thinks negative thoughts in reaction to events around him (e.g., Woody Allen characters, Jerry Seinfeld). Discern what the character is worried about. Create alternative thoughts the character could have in reaction to the events around him.

Awareness of adverse events and how one thinks about their consequences: Not catastrophizing. Explain to students that people can choose to react positively or negatively to adverse events and that how one thinks about the event and others' actions will affect the outcome of the event. Emphasize to students the importance of not only thinking about the worst case scenario but also the best case scenario. Present an adverse event to the students (either a simple adverse event like the one below, or a larger, real-life community-oriented event) and have them brainstorm about what the worst and best case scenarios could be. Discuss with the students what would happen if the character only thought about the worst case scenario. Example of an adverse event: I had a birthday party at my house and invited 10 of my friends. After we ate cake, several of my friends started whispering and wouldn't tell me what they were saying.

Coping by Applying Positive Reasoning
Ideas for Developing Skills

Level 2: Attention to Facts and Skills
Focus on detail and prototypical knowledge, Build knowledge

Understanding how to give others the "benefit of the doubt."
Define the meaning of giving others "the benefit of the doubt." Explain to students that giving other people the benefit of the doubt is one type of positive thinking. Present hypothetical situations to students (e.g., being "accidentally" pushed by another student who has made fun of you in the past) and ask students to role play giving "the benefit of the doubt" to the other student rather than accusing him/her of lying or pushing him/her back.

Understanding positive thinking in conflicts. Most people think all conflicts are negative, and when in conflict, think negatively about others or self. Emphasize to students that conflicts can be good; they can actually strengthen relationships and friendships and contribute to positive feelings about oneself and others. For conflicts to be good the people in the conflict need to have positive thinking. They need to want to maintain a good relationship with the other person, be willing to work with the other person to resolve the conflict, and not think negatively about the other person or oneself. Find examples of conflicts in movies or books (e.g., the movie *Stand by Me*) or a community problem that involved positive thinking. Discuss with students how the characters in the book/movie or community members were positive about their conflicts in any way. Point out the intricacy of how someone can be angry with another person and still think about him/her positively at the same time. If using a community problem, ask a community member who has positive thinking to talk about the conflict and people's attitudes during the conflict.

Scavenger hunt of positive thinking. Set up an activity with staff in the school building. Have students work in groups to gather a list of positive comments from staff in the building. For example, they have to identify who corresponds to statements like these: "I help you to think about yourself in a positive way (Counselor). "I help you make positive choices for good health" (PE instructor, or kitchen cook). Students have to go to the person and find out if their guess is correct. The staff member is to give students a positive statement or aphorism—that the staff member values—to write down (e.g., "Look at the sunny side of life" or "Every cloud has a silver lining"). Use 5-10 staff/statements. Ask students to reflect on their responses to the positive statements.

Lookout Week. Have students find examples of negative thinking in the news and in their lives. Assign them to keep a record and report the negative thinking they observe. When they turn in their reports, choose some examples of negative thinking that they identified and present them to the class. As a group, brainstorm alternative ways to think about each of these examples.

Starred ★ activities
within each subskill
go together!

EJ-7 Coping

Coping by Applying Positive Reasoning
Ideas for Developing Skills

Level 2 (continued)

Countering catastrophic thinking. Give students specific questions and cues to help them counter catastrophic thoughts (i.e., thinking only about the worst case scenario). Present an adverse event to the students (either a simple adverse event like the one below, or a larger, real-life community-oriented event). Use the following questions (from Seligman's, 1995, *The Optimistic Child*) to have students answer after reading various adverse situations: (1) What is the worst thing that might happen? (2) What is one thing that the individual can do to stop the worst thing from happening? (3) What is the best thing that could happen? (4) What is one thing that the individual can do to help make the best thing happen? (5) What is the most likely thing that will happen? (6) What can the individual do to handle the most likely thing if it happens? Example scenarios (from Seligman's, 1995, *The Optimistic Child*) include:

- Sandra's mom told her that she expected Sandra to clean the bathroom by the time she got home from work. When Sandra's mom gets home, she sees the bathroom is a mess and Sandra is outside playing.
- Joe is fifteen and likes a particular girl. His friends convince him to ask her out. He manages to get up the guts, and when he asks her, she says no.
- Jackie's parents are fighting a lot. She lies in bed at night and listens to them yell at each other. It seems as if they are fighting more each day.

Level 3: Practice Procedures
Set goals, Plan steps of problem solving, Practice skills

Individual practice in giving others the "benefit of the doubt." After students have learned what giving others the benefit of the doubt is, ask them to practice doing this with others over the next week. Have them keep a journal, identifying and describing situations in which they have given others the benefit of the doubt (or could/should have).

Using positive thinking in conflicts. Once students have learned how they can be positive during conflicts, ask them to practice this in their relationships with peers, friends, and family. Have them keep a journal, identifying conflicts that they have had with others. Ask them to describe their positive thoughts during the conflict, or positive thoughts they could have had during the conflict.

Read nonfiction positive thinking guides. Students read such books as Peale's (1952) *The Power of Positive Thinking* (or excerpts from these types of books) and practice one or more techniques suggested. **Assess** by having students write a report on what technique they used and whether they found it helpful or not and why.

Starred ★ activities within each subskill go together!

Coping by Applying Positive Reasoning
Ideas for Developing Skills

Level 3 (continued)

Diagnosing negative thinking. Select (carefully) examples of negative thinking on television shows, in movies or books. Have students work in groups to suggest positive ways the characters could have thought about the situation.

Negative thinking in pop music. Have students evaluate the words of the music they listen to. Ask students to write a report about their evaluations. Instruct them to include in their report whether the words are positive or negative. If there are positive words, describe what is positive, and if the words are negative, describe how the words can be changed to be more positive.

Practicing decatastrophic thinking. Ask students to identify adverse events over the next two weeks and write them in a journal. Instruct them to then answer the following questions (from Seligman's, 1995, *The Optimistic Child*) for each adverse situation in order to practice decatastrophic thinking: (1) What is the worst thing that might happen? (2) What is one thing that the individual can do to stop the worst thing from happening? (3) What is the best thing that could happen? (4) What is one thing that the individual can do to help make the best thing happen? (5) What is the most likely thing that will happen? (6) What can the individual do to handle the most likely thing if it happens?

Countering negative messages from friends and family. Have students evaluate the messages they get about life from their family and friends. Using a journal, ask students to identify these messages and then describe how they would change them to be positive. Also ask students to write how they could verbally respond back to the negative message with a positive one and then communicate this response to the other person.

Test your optimism/pessimism. Have students test their optimism/pessimism at http://discoveryhealth.queendom.com. Use the information to design a class plan to increase optimism in the class members.

Level 4: Integrate Knowledge and Procedures
Execute plans, Solve problems

Mentoring others in positive attitudes. Assign students a younger student who needs assistance in learning a particular social skill. Prepare the older students carefully to ensure that they keep a positive attitude throughout their interaction with the younger student and help the younger student think positive thoughts about learning the social skill.

Puppet show. Have students write a puppet show or a children's book for younger students in which they demonstrate how to decatastrophize and think positively. Have students give the show, or read the book, to younger students.

Assessment Hints

Applying positive reasoning

Use multiple-choice, true-false, and short answer tests to assess students' knowledge of positive thinking skills (e.g., giving others the benefit of the doubt, being positive during a conflict with another person, what catastrophic and decatastrophic thinking is and what the decatastrophizing thought process is).

Use media clips or written scenarios that have negative thoughts and have students identify the negative thoughts and write positive thoughts.

Provide a description of an adverse situation. Have the student respond to it describing both the best case and worst case scenario (Level 1) or answer the 6 decatastrophizing questions (Level 3).

EJ-7 Coping

Coping by Managing Disappointment and Failure

Creative and Expert Implementer Real-Life Example

Former President **Richard Nixon** successfully managed disappointment and failure before he became President of the United States. He lost two big elections before winning the presidential election in 1968. In 1960, he ran for President against John F. Kennedy, in which he lost. In 1962, he ran for governor of California and lost. In 1968, Nixon ran for President again and won this time, becoming the 37th President of the United States.

Ideas for Developing Skills

Starred ★ activities within each subskill go together!

Level 1: Immersion in Examples and Opportunities
Attend to the big picture, Learn to recognize basic patterns

Awareness of adverse events and how one thinks about them: Attributions. Explain to students that people can choose to react positively or negatively to adverse events and that how one thinks about the event and others' actions can affect the outcome of the event. Emphasize to students the importance of identifying one's beliefs about the event and changing negative beliefs to positive beliefs. Present examples of adverse events and various consequences (either a simple adverse event like the one below, or a larger, real-life community oriented event). Have students brainstorm about what the beliefs might be for each consequence. Examples include:

Adverse event: I had a birthday party at my house and invited 10 of my friends. After we ate cake, several of my friends started whispering and wouldn't tell me what they were saying.
Consequence 1: I got really mad and told them all to leave.
Consequence 2: I ignored them and announced that I'm now going to open presents.
Consequence 3: I smiled at them and turned to another friend and whispered something in his ear.

Discuss with the students which consequence and corresponding belief is the most positive and why it's better than the other consequences.

Noticing irrational beliefs. Present examples of the 10 beliefs (listed on the left) to the students (from film/tv/video excerpts, books, stories, real life, etc.). Present them (or an alternative set) a week later and see if the students can identify correctly which belief is demonstrated.

Managing personal failure. Discuss with students how individuals feel like failures for different reasons, depending on what you think is important (your values) and what you expect of yourself. (a) Find examples of people who think they are failures but others don't see them that way. Imagine what their values are that they are not meeting. (b) Find examples of people who have failed personally (e.g., divorce, abuse of others, drug addiction) and started over. Learn their stories. What did they do to turn themselves around? What did they need as support?

IRRATIONAL BELIEFS

1. Everything should go my way and I should always get what I want.
2. The world should be fair, and bad people should be punished.
3. Things should come easily for me.
4. I shouldn't show my feelings (I must be in complete control).
5. I shouldn't have to wait for anything.
6. I must win.
7. It's awful if other people don't like me.
8. There is only one right answer.
9. I'm bad if I make a mistake.
10. Adults should be perfect.

Coping by Managing Disappointment and Failure
Ideas for Developing Skills

Level 1 (continued)

Managing occupational failure. Find examples of persons failing at a career (e.g., President Truman before he was president). Discuss what can lead to failure: mismatch of talent/skill and the requirements of the job, lack of effort required, lack of motivation, family distractions, war, bad luck, etc. Discuss how people cope with occupational failure and the causes of failure.

Managing failure at school. Discuss reasons people might fail at school (e.g., too many responsibilities at home and no time for homework, lack of motivation, lack of basic skills, lack of understanding the purpose of schooling). Discuss ways that students and their families can overcome the obstacles to success.

Dealing with disappointment. Discuss with students how individuals can feel disappointed for different reasons. Discuss ways to deal with disappointment immediately (e.g., distract yourself with something else to do, talk to a friend or family member about it) and long-term (decide if you want to try again and break down the steps you need to take into baby steps; if you don't want to try again, select something that you will take better care of). Give students examples of disappointments and ask them to write healthy reactions to them and to make plans for change.

Assuming the worst. Sometimes we upset ourselves when we catastrophize or assume the worst about something. Woody Allen often plays characters who react like this much of the time. (a) Find examples of catastrophizing in movies, tv, stories, real life. Have students reframe the catastrophizing into more realistic conceptions. (b) When something goes wrong in the classroom, have students give a range of reactions, from catastrophizing to realistic response to minimizing. Have them, in the end, constructively respond.

Level 2: Attention to Facts and Skills
Focus on detail and prototypical examples, Build knowledge

Starred ★ activities within each subskill go together!

Finding irrational beliefs. Have students find examples of a selected subset of irrational beliefs from the list according to (a) those that fit in a particular subject matter or material; (b) those commonly seen in the community; (c) those commonly seen in favorite entertainment. Present them to class. Discuss more appropriate ways of thinking about and handling the situation.

Recovering irrational believers. Invite persons from 12-step programs to talk to the class about how they overcome irrational beliefs.

Coping by Managing Disappointment and Failure
Ideas for Developing Skills

Level 2 (continued)

How to think positively about adverse situations. Positive or negative reactions to adverse situations greatly depend on the thought processes of the person. Individuals who react negatively to adverse situations often have automatic negative thoughts. They do not question whether these negative thoughts could be inaccurate, and they act on the negative thoughts, which often results in negative consequences. To help students react positively to adverse situations, explain to them that they need to be conscious of their thought process when encountering adverse situations. They can learn to think positively about adverse situations when they catch their automatic thoughts (i.e., acknowledging that their automatic thoughts are not necessarily accurate), and generate more accurate explanations. Present examples of adverse situations to the students (either a simple adverse situation like the one below, or a larger, real-life community oriented situation) and go through each of the above steps. Example adverse situations include:

- My friend has been snapping back at me a lot lately.
- It's the first week of eighth grade and I don't feel like anybody likes me.
- My best friend got an invitation to another friend's party, but I didn't.

Reacting positively to challenging events. Brainstorm with students what kinds of positive things you might say to yourself when something goes wrong. For example: Maybe it's just an accident. Maybe I took it the wrong way. Time for a few deep breaths. I'm going to keep my cool and let the other guy get himself into trouble. Chill out. I can't expect people to act the way that I want them to. Plan ahead. Post each item on the wall (on separate sheets). When something goes wrong, or when someone in the class catastrophizes, point to one of the statements.

The lenses we use. In *Life Strategies for Teens*, Jay McGraw (2000) discusses how all of us have lenses through which we see the world. We evaluate everything that happens to us according to the lens we wear. If we don't live up to the demands of the lens, we feel worthless. He identifies the following lenses: the Me lens, the Peer lens, the I'm in love lens (requiring you to always have a boyfriend or girlfriend), material (consumer), achievement, authority (gaining their approval or disapproval), victim, hate, safety. The lens you wear affects your perceptions and judgments of others and judgments about yourself. (1) Read or watch a story about a person whose attitude affects how people react to him or her and how the person reacts to events. Have students identify the lens the character is using. (2) Have students discuss a situation and how people with different lenses might interpret it (e.g., someone cuts in front of you in line, or a parent grounds you). (3) Have students look for examples of lenses for a period of time and record what they notice.

Starred ★ activities within each subskill go together!

Coping by Managing Disappointment and Failure
Ideas for Developing Skills

Level 2 (continued)

Responding constructively to failure (Gibbs, Potter, & Goldstein, 1995). Use the following steps in discussing failure: (a) Recall your goal and decide if you really failed. (b) Figure out why you failed—what errors did you make, what circumstances contributed. (c) Figure out what you could do differently next time. (d) Decide if you want to try again or get another chance and do better. (e) If appropriate, make a plan to try again. Here are some situations that to which you can apply this skill: failing a test, a project you've worked on a long time doesn't come out right, your girl/boyfriend says he or she wants to break up, you didn't finish your homework, you wanted to make 10 baskets but you only made 8.

Rational beliefs. Here is a set of beliefs that people in recovery programs try to learn and apply in their lives on a daily basis. Post them in class and point them out as important tools for living a satisfying life. (1) Everybody doesn't have to love me. (2) It is okay to make mistakes. (3) Other people are okay and I am okay. (4) I don't have to control things. Things will work out. (5) I am responsible for my day. (6) I can handle it when things go wrong. (7) It is important to try. (8) I am capable. (9) I can change. (10) Other people are capable. I can care about them but I can't solve their problems. (11) I can be flexible. (12) I can make a contribution.

Level 3: Practice Procedures
Set goals, Plan steps of problem solving, Practice skills

Practicing positive thinking about adverse situations. Have students in small groups generate their adverse situations through quick brainstorming. Have students respond to them by identifying an automatic negative thought and the likely consequence of the negative thought. Also have them respond to the adverse situation and the consequence of what's decided using the steps below. Have each group role play the two versions of their adverse situations for the rest of the class.
- What is my automatic negative thought?
- What is the belief behind my negative thought?
- What is the evidence for and against my belief?
- What are some other ways of seeing the situation?
- Are any of these other ways more accurate explanations?
- Which is the most accurate way of seeing the situation?

Personal Recovery. Students identify irrational beliefs that they have and work on eradicating them one at a time. Keep a journal and write in it whenever the irrational belief arises. Then dialogue (in the journal) with the irrational belief to counter and defeat it.

Starred ★ activities
within each subskill
go together!

Coping by Managing
Disappointment and Failure
Ideas for Developing Skills

Level 3 (continued)

What lens do you use? Create activities based on the activity "The lenses we use." Then follow with lots of experience on identifying lenses in others in various situations. When they are comfortable with this, have them write about how they would personally respond to vignettes that you present.

How do you think and feel? Discuss with students what the choices are in thinking about situations that are disappointing. Point out the relation between thinking a particular way and the feeling that corresponds to it. Here are examples of situations that you might use for discussion: (a) someone disappoints you (friend, family, leader, team); (b) you fail at something you were expected to do (obligation); (c) you fail at something you wanted to do; (d) you fail at something you needed to do; (e) you didn't win; (f) you aren't winning; (g) you hear a rumor that someone doesn't like you; (h) people don't like your opinions; (i) people don't like what you do/did.

Where does this feeling come from? Discuss how negative feelings often stem from what you are thinking. Why do you feel humiliated when you do? Why do you feel angry when you do?

Learn from failure. Students should reflect on their failure so they can improve for the next time. (1) Was the failure under my control or was it beyond my control? (2) Was I prepared enough? How can I better prepare myself? (3) Was I too anxious? How can I overcome my anxiety and not 'choke up?' (4) Who can I consult for help with my performance? (5) What is one step I will take to better prepare myself?

Level 4: Integrate Knowledge and Procedures
Execute plans, Solve problems

Monitoring positive thinking about own adverse situations. Have students keep track of the adverse situations that they experience over a period of time. Have them respond to the adverse situation using the steps in the Level 3 activity, "Practicing Positive Thinking about Adverse Situations," p. 134. Ask them to describe the situation, the process they used to respond to it, and the outcome of the situation in a journal.

Mentored change. Ask recovering adults to mentor students in overcoming irrational beliefs. Ask the adults to gauge their progress after a set amount of time (at least a month).

Starred ⭐ activities within each subskill go together!

Coping by Managing Disappointment and Failure
Ideas for Developing Skills

Level 4 (continued)

Mentoring change. Have students mentor someone younger in changing irrational beliefs as they apply to school.

Being coached. Have students select an area where they need to work on dealing with disappointment or failure. Have them select a mentor in this area (e.g., older teammate on a sport team). Have students keep track of their progress in a journal where they report the incident and how they felt and how they acted. Ask the mentor to coach them. After a period of time, ask the mentor to evaluate their progress.

Coaching others. Have students mentor a younger child who is dealing with disappointment or failure. Give the students concrete activities to do to make the interactions successful.

Assessment Hints

Mangaing Disappointment and Failure

Provide a description of an adverse situation with multiple consequences. Have the student respond to it describing both the beliefs behind each consequence (Level 1).

Provide a description of an adverse situation. Ask students to write their automatic thoughts, evaluate the accuracy of these thoughts, and generate other explanations that would be more accurate (Level 2).

Provide a description of an adverse situation. Ask students to answer the questions detailed in the Level 3 activity.

Assess journal entries when journaling is part of the activity.

Creative and Expert Implementer Real-Life Example

Coping by Developing Resilience

Helen Keller was born blind and deaf but through hard work and relentless effort she finished college, wrote over a dozen books, became an international speaker, and received the Presidential Medal of Freedom (the highest honor a civilian can receive).

Ideas for Developing Skills

Level 1: Immersion in Examples and Opportunities
Attend to the big picture, Learn to recognize basic patterns

What is resilience? (1) Discuss the nature of resiliency. Resilience is the ability to cope positively with life stressors such as family problems, health problems, community problems. It is the ability to succeed despite adversity, tragedy or trauma like physical abuse, sexual abuse, or extreme poverty. (2) Have students find examples of people who are resilient. Look for successful people in various fields who have overcome serious background handicaps.

What resilient people have. A combination of factors contributes to resilience. Many studies show that the primary factor in resilience is having caring and supportive relationships within and outside the family. Relationships that create love and trust, provide role models, and offer encouragement and reassurance help bolster a person's resilience. Several additional factors are associated with resilience. Have students rate themselves on each of these here or use the Search Institute's inventory of assets. Personal (internal) qualities: (a) Ability to make a plan and carry it out; (b) Positive view of yourself; (c) Confidence in your abilities; (d) Belief in your strength; (e) Ability to communicate well with others (family, friends, strangers); (f) Ability to solve problems; (g) Ability to manage anger; (h) Ability to manage your impulses. Social (external) qualities: (a) Caring relationship with at least one adult; (b) Someone who loves you; (c) An adult role model; (d) A relationship that encourages and supports you.

Level 2: Attention to Facts and Skills
Focus on detail and prototypical knowledge, Build knowledge

Resiliency quizzes. (1) Have students go the resiliency website and take the two quizzes to find out how resilient they are. (2) Have students select an area in which to develop resiliency based on the quiz results.

Starred ★ activities within each subskill go together!

Coping
by Developing Resilience
Ideas for Developing Skills

Level 2 (continued)

Coping skills test. Coping refers to our attempts to manage external and internal demands or stress; it includes our thoughts, attitudes, skills and actions. We estimate our abilities to cope based on what we remember from previous experience in similar situations, how much knowledge we have about coping, our sense of self-confidence and risk-taking in general, how well we think our personal coping skills compare to others', and how much faith we have in getting support from others (Holroyd & Lazarus, 1982). Have students test their coping skills at http://discoveryhealth.queendom. com. You can use the test questions for discussion and use the test scores to motivate the students to improve their scores.

Develop resiliency by changing your thinking towards stressful

events. Have students practice changing their thinking. (1) When an unexpected problem occurs, don't look at it as "ruining everything." Instead, think about what other options you have (think outside the box) and look forward to the future being better. (2) When a goal you had is no longer possible (e.g., you wanted to be a basketball star but you are too short), accept the circumstances and think about other things you like. (3) See the big picture and how the stressful event fits into a lifetime of events. (4) Be optimistic. Imagine what you want to do. Have students practice using these mental transformations with a list of stressful outcomes. (5) Take an action. Try to do something about the problem or find a new outlet for your energy. For example, (a) You get a B on a test, making your class grade an A- instead of the A you wanted. (b) You break your leg and can't play in the championship game. (c) Your purse is stolen. (d) you lose your backpack of school books. (e) Your boy/girlfriend breaks up with you.

A good sense of humor. Laughing is a stress reliever and a way to relax

the body. It is an important way to cope with blunders and things out of one's control. Help students develop a good sense of humor. Use websites like www.ahajokes.com (only clean jokes) or http://www.kidsjokes.co.uk/ or kidhumor.glowport.com to bring up at least one joke per day. Other sites with links:
www.jokes2000.com
Science jokes: http://www.xs4all.nl/~jcdverha/scijokes/
Musical instrument jokes: http://www.mit.edu/~jcb/jokes/
Math jokes: http://www.ahajokes.com/math_jokes.html
Economy/economists jokes: http://netec.mcc.ac.uk/JokEc.html

Coping
by Developing Resilience
Ideas for Developing Skills

Level 3: Practice Procedures
Set goals, Plan steps of problem solving, Practice skills

Develop resiliency by nurturing good relationships. Have students assess how supportive their relationships are and make a relationship web. Good relationships are critical to resiliency. These relationships are often found in family members or friends. But they can also be found in community groups like church groups, recovery groups or civic groups. Groups like these are especially helpful in helping one to regain hope after a difficult loss. Bad relationships can be harmful to resiliency (see more at www.resiliency.com).

Develop resiliency by reflecting on your strengths. Often, people who have difficult lives hear only bad things about themselves and have never thought about what is good about them. Have students identify their strengths and make a bookmark, poster or card to themselves that lists their strengths.

1. What stressful events have I faced in my life? Which ones are the most difficult for me?
2. How have these events affected me?
3. What has helped me get through these events? Relationships? Support group? Religion? Religious community?
4. What do I know about myself from these experiences?
5. Have I helped someone else get through a similar event? If so, did it help me?
6. What obstacles did I overcome and how did I do that?
7. What makes me feel more positive about the future?

Avoid perfectionism. There are several things that people do to avoid perfectionism. Give your students something difficult to do that they won't succeed at and have them practice doing the following. (1) Tell yourself it's okay to make a mistake. In fact, give yourself a break and allow yourself to make several mistakes a day. (2) Learn from role models about how to turn around a mistake. (3) Study the mistakes that famous people have made. For example, how many materials did Thomas Edison try out to make the light-bulb? Babe Ruth made the most homeruns and the most strikeouts in the same year. (4) Say positive things to yourself (e.g., "Everything is fine. I will survive."). (5) When you make a mistake, don't tell yourself that you are stupid, tell yourself that you need to work harder. (6) When you make a mistake, figure out what to do differently next time.

Coping
by Developing Resilience
Ideas for Developing Skills

Level 4: Integrate Knowledge and Procedures
Execute plans, Solve problems

Develop resiliency with self nurturance. People can develop resilience by maintaining a positive image of themselves, by taking care of themselves like they would a good friend, by exploring who they are in positive ways, by training their finer instincts and learning to trust their inner self. There are several activities that support resilience: regular exercise, regular deep relaxation, healthy eating, spending time with loved ones who are supportive. Have students design a plan for themselves and keep a diary about their progress.

Develop resiliency by helping others. Helping others helps a person feel valued and worthwhile. It is an opportunity to connect with others. Ask students to volunteer in a social/civic/religious organization. Discourage middle school students from working with the disadvantaged because research shows that, for them, stereotypes are reinforced. Have students keep a journal.

Develop resiliency by using resources. People who nurture resiliency in themselves know they sometimes need help from others and from other resources. (1) Have students identify resources that are helpful to nurturing resilience. (2) Have students create posters to hang around the school with this information. (3) Have students create a resiliency guide that includes this information. (4) Hand out the resiliency guide to other students.

Develop resiliency through problem solving. Develop a plan for taking steps towards your goals. Have students list the goals they have for their lives. Have them develop a plan for reaching their goals. Break the plan into small enough steps that they can accomplish a step every day or every week. Have students keep track of their progress.

Take the Resiliency Quiz (www.resiliency.com/htm/resiliencyquiz.htm). Have students take the Resiliency Quiz (you can make copies) and then select one or two of the resiliency "builders" to work on. Have them report weekly on their progress.

Inform others about resiliency. Design and carry out a campaign to inform other students and community members about the importance of resiliency and how to support each other in its development.

EJ-7 Coping

Assessment Hints

Developing resilience

Have students complete reflective activities such as writing essays or keeping a report diary on their own resilience.

Have students participate in various forms of communications such as reports, posters, public service announcements, or speeches on what is resilience and how to support each other in its development.

Create a Climate
to Develop Coping Skills

The development of optimism is related to the resolution of past experiences. For example, if a student has had difficulty in the past having his basic needs met (e.g., food, shelter) he may be less hopeful that the future will bring happiness and that people have beneficent motives.

To counter students' reinforced pessimistic attitudes, <u>model</u> an optimistic explanatory style to your students and <u>encourage</u> them to think in these ways: (from Seligman, 1995)

Personal optimistic explanations	Examples
Good events have permanent causes.	"Beth won the geography bee because she's a hard worker and studies for her geography class."
Bad events have temporary causes.	"It takes time to find new friends when you change schools."
Bad events have temporary explanations.	"I stink at math" (vs. "I stink at school" or "I'm not smart").
Good events have global explanations.	"Jerome got to play Peter Pan because he's got a lot of talent" (vs. "Jerome got to play Peter Pan because he's a good singer").
When something negative happens to you and it's your fault, it's due to temporary, specific, and internal causes.	"I got a D on the test because I didn't study hard enough" (vs. "... because I'm stupid"). "I did not make the basketball team because I'm not good at basketball" (vs. "... because the coach doesn't like me").

When you criticize your students, use temporary explanations that are specific to the situation.

When you hear other students use permanent, global criticisms of others ("He flunked his science test ... he's so dumb!), intervene to offer and argue a more temporary and specific explanation of the negative event ("He did not do well on his science test because he didn't pay attention in class for the last two weeks and didn't study").

Be open about some of your disappointments and failures. Model to the students appropriate ways to approach them.

Encourage students to refocus themselves after failure and disappointment. Encourage students to encourage each other.

Sample Student Self-Monitoring
Coping

Encourage active learning by having students learn to monitor their own learning

Applying positive reasoning

When someone does something wrong to me or someone else that's question-
ably accidental or out of their control, I give him/her the benefit of the
doubt.

When something goes wrong, I know it will work out eventually.

Things usually work out when I try something for the first time.

When one thing goes wrong, other things are still okay.

When something goes wrong, I think of the good things that can/will
happen.

When something goes wrong, I think of the best case scenario that could
happen.

When something goes wrong, I think of how I can change it to make it right.

When something goes wrong, I try to be realistic about what is most likely to
happen.

Managing Disappointment and Failure

I try to catch my automatic thoughts when I encounter a negative situation.

I evaluate my automatic thoughts when encountering a negative situation.

I try to generate accurate explanations of why the negative situation happened.

I can accept failure and make plans to try again.

I don't believe I have to be good at everything.

It's okay to be bad at some things.

When I fail, I try harder in smarter ways.

Developing Resilience

I am aware of the assets that contribute to a successful life.

I know which areas of resiliency I need to work on.

I know steps to take to build resiliency skills.

I work on building resiliency skills every day.

Selections to Post in the Classroom
For Coping

Live a long life:
Lessons from survivors
of concentration camps
(from Johnson, 1993)

1. Maintain deep commitments and goals.
2. Share your distress with others.
3. Keep your morale high.
4. Stay physically active.
5. Maintain friendships and love relationships.

Selections to Post in the Classroom
For Coping

As humans, we can try to explain to ourselves
why something bad happened:

The problem we are having will not last forever.

Optimism is a skill.

Being optimistic leads to more success in life.

Look for the good intention in others.

Selections to Post in the Classroom
For Coping

Resilient Thoughts

1. Everybody doesn't have to love me.
2. It is okay to make mistakes.
3. Other people are okay and I am okay.
4. I don't have to control things. Things will work out.
5. I am responsible for my day.
6. I can handle it when things go wrong.
7. It is important to try.
8. I am capable.
9. I can change.
10. Other people are capable. I can care about them but I can't solve their problems.
11. I can be flexible.
12. I can make a contribution.

Ethical Judgment Appendix

Lesson Planning Guide

'Linking to the Community' Worksheet

Rubric Examples
    Journaling
    Papers or Reports
    Group Project

Special Activities
    Cognitive Apprenticeship
    Cooperative Learning
    Guidelines for Cross-Age Tutoring
    Reciprocal Teaching
    Ethical Dilemma Discussion
    The Jigsaw Method
    Structured Controversy

Making a Strategic Plan for Change

Linking EJ Skills to Search Institute Assets

Recommended Resources for Character Education

Resources/References for Ethical Judgment
    Ethical Dilemma Resources with sample dilemma
    Book References Cited in Ethical Judgment Activities
    Citizenship Resources
    References Cited in Booklet

Lesson Planning Guide

1. **Select an ethical category and identify the subskill you will address in your lesson(s).**

2. **Select a graduation standard or academic requirement and identify the sub-components.**

3. **Match up the ethical sub-skill with the academic sub-components.**

4. **Generate lesson activities using these elements:**

   (a) Enlist the communities resources.
   (For ideas, consult the Linking to Community worksheet, pp. 154-159)

   (b) Focus on a variety of teaching styles and intelligences.
   Teaching styles: Visual, Auditory, Tactile, Kinesthetic, Oral, Individual/Cooperative, Olfactory, Gustatory, Spatial

   Intelligences: Musical, Bodily-Kinesthetic, Spatial Logico-Mathematical, Linguistic, Interpersonal, Intrapersonal

   (c) Identify questions that you can ask that promote different kinds of thinking and memory.

   Creative Thinking

   Prospective Thinking

   Retrospective Thinking

   Motivational Thinking

   Practical Thinking

   Types of Memory:

   > Autobiographical (personal experience)

   > Narrative (storyline)

   > Procedural (how to)

   > Semantic (what)

5. **Create an activity for each <u>level of expertise</u> you will address (worksheet provided on next page). Indicate which activities fit with which lesson. For each activity, indicate how you will <u>assess learning</u>.**

Lesson Planning Guide
(continued)

<u>ACTIVITY</u>   <u>STUDENT ASSESSMENT</u>

Level 1: Immersion in Examples and Opportunities
(Attend to the big picture, Learn to recognize basic patterns)

Level 2: Attention to Facts and Skills
(Focus on detail and prototypical examples, Build knowledge)

Level 3: Practice Procedures
(Set goals, Plan steps of problem solving, Practice skills)

Level 4: Integrate Knowledge and Procedures
(Execute plans, Solve problems)

Ethical Judgment Appendix

CHECKLIST FOR
Linking to the Community

What resources must be accessed for learning the skill or subskill?

What resources must be identified to successfully complete the skill or subskill?

1. SOCIAL NETWORK RESOURCES

Circle the resources that must be accessed for learning the skill:

Family____   Friendship____   Service group____

Neighborhood____   Social groups ____   Community____

City____   Park & Rec____   State____

National ____   International____

Other:_____Other:_____

On the line next to each circled item, indicate the <u>manner of contact</u>:

Contact in person (P), by telephone (T)

2. SEMANTIC KNOWLEDGE RESOURCES

Circle the resources that must be accessed for learning the skill:

Books and other library sources____   Web____

Librarians____   Educators and Intellectuals____

Business leaders____   Community experts____

Other:_____   Other:_____

On the line next to each circled item, indicate the <u>manner of contact</u>:

Contact in person (P), Email (E), Web (W), Letter (L), Telephone (T)

CHECKLIST FOR
Linking to the Community
(continued)

3. AUTHORITY STRUCTURE RESOURCES

Circle the resources that must be accessed for learning the skill:

School officials____   Government officials (all levels) ____ United Nations____

Other Leaders:_____

_____

_____

Indicate the manner of contact for each item:

Contact in person (P), Telephone (T), Letter (L), Email (E)

4. ORGANIZATIONAL RESOURCES

What types of organizations can give guidance?

_____

_____

_____

_____

How can they help?

_____

_____

_____

_____

_____

_____

_____

_____

_____

Ethical Judgment Appendix

CHECKLIST FOR
Linking to the Community
(continued)

5. **AGE GROUP RESOURCES**

   Circle the resources that must be accessed for learning the skill:

   - Teen groups in various community organizations_____

        Specify:

   - School groups_____

        Specify:

   - Senior citizen groups_____

        Specify:

   - Children's groups_____

        Specify:

   - Women's groups_____

        Specify:

   - Men's groups_____

        Specify:

   Indicate the manner of contact for each circled item:

   Contact in person (P), Telephone (T), Letter (L), Email (E)

CHECKLIST FOR
Linking to the Community
(continued)

6. MATERIAL RESOURCES

Types of Materials

- scraps (from scrap yards)

- second-hand (from second-hand stores, recycling places)

- new

- handmade

Identify the resources that must be accessed for learning the skill:

What materials do you need for your project?

_____

_____

_____

Where can you get it?

_____

_____

_____

How can you get it?

_____

_____

_____

Indicate the manner of contact for each item:

Contact in person (P), Telephone (T), Letter (L), Email (E)

CHECKLIST FOR
Linking to the Community
(continued)

7. EXPERTISE RESOURCES

Types of Expertise

social networking _____   design_____   musical _____

physical (game/sport, dance) _____   creating_____   knowledge _____

finance_____   selling _____

Identify the resources that must be accessed for learning the skill:

What expertise is required?

_____

_____

_____

_____

Who has expertise?

_____

_____

Can I develop expertise or must I depend on an expert?

_____

_____

Who can help me figure out what to do?

_____

_____

_____

Indicate the manner of contact for each item:

Telephone (T), Take a class (C), Contact in person (P), Book (B)

CHECKLIST FOR
Linking to the Community
(continued)

8. FINANCIAL RESOURCES

Circle the sources that must be accessed for learning the skill:

Grants____   Loans____   Donors____

Earn money____

Bartering (use library and experts to find these out) ____

Indicate the manner of contact for each circled item:

Contact in person (P), Telephone (T), Letter (L), Email (E)

9. PERSONAL RESOURCES

What abilities and skills do I have that I can use to reach the goal?

_____

_____

_____

_____

10. OTHER RESOURCES

What other resources might be needed or are optional?

_____

_____

_____

_____

Rubric Examples

GUIDES FOR CREATING YOUR OWN RUBRIC

Creating Rubrics
(Blueprint of behavior for peak or acceptable level of performance)

❖ Establish Learner Outcome goals
❖ Cluster these characteristics
❖ Determine which combinations of characteristics show
   Unsatisfactory, Satisfactory, Excellent 'job'
❖ Create examples of work showing different levels of performance
❖ List expectations on a form
❖ Present criteria to students ahead of time

RUBRIC FOR JOURNALING

Quality of Journaling		
Content: Quantity Few requirements for content are covered. 0 1 2 3	Most requirements are included fairly well. 4 5 6 7	Content requirements are thoroughly covered. 8 9 10
Content: Type Rarely are thoughts included in entries. 0 1 2 3	Sometimes thoughts are included in entries. 4 5 6 7	Thoughts are consistently included in entries. 8 9 10
Content: Clarity Entries are difficult to understand. 0 1 2 3	Entries can be understood with some effort. 4 5 6 7	Entries are easily understood. 8 9 10

Rubric Examples (continued)

RUBRIC FOR PAPERS OR REPORTS

Qualities of Paper or Written Report		
Organization The paper is difficult to follow. 0 1 2 3	The paper is easy to follow and read. 4 5 6 7	All relationships among ideas are clearly expressed by the sentence structures and word choices. 8 9 10
Writing Style The style of the writing is sloppy, has no clear direction, looks like it was written by several people. 0 1 2 3	The format is appropriate with correct spelling, good grammar, good punctuation and appropriate transition sentences. 4 5 6 7	The paper is well written and is appropriate for presentation in the firm. 8 9 10
Content The paper has no point. The ideas are aimless, disconnected. 0 1 2 3	The paper makes a couple of clear points but weakly, with few supportive facts. 4 5 6 7	The paper makes one or two strong points. Support for these arguments is well described. 8 9 10

Ethical Judgment Appendix

Rubric Examples (continued)

RUBRIC FOR GROUP PROJECT
(Bloomer & Lutz as cited in Walvoord & Anderson, 1998)

Evaluation of a Group Project*	Rating
Comprehension: Seemed to understand requirements for assignment.	0 1 2 3 Not Observed
Problem Identification and Solution: Participated in identifying and defining problems and working towards a solution.	0 1 2 3 Not Observed
Organization: Approached tasks (such as time management) in systematic way.	0 1 2 3 Not Observed
Acceptance of responsibility: Took responsibility for assigned tasks in the project.	0 1 2 3 Not Observed
Initiative/motivation: Made suggestions, sought feedback, showed interest in group decision making and planning.	0 1 2 3 Not Observed
Creativity: Considered ideas from unusual or different viewpoints.	0 1 2 3 Not Observed
Task completion: Followed through in completing own contributions to the group project.	0 1 2 3 Not Observed
Attendance: Attended planning sessions, was prompt and participated in decision making.	0 1 2 3 Not Observed

Add Total Score   Total:_____

Divide by number of items scored with a number   Average:_____

Comments:

Special Activities

COGNITIVE APPRENTICESHIP
(Collins, Hawkins, & Carver, 1991, p. 228)

Teach *process* (how to) and *provide guided experience* in cognitive skills.

Teach *content* relevant to the task.

Teach this content for each subject area:

Strategic knowledge: how to work successfully in the subject area

Domain knowledge: the kind of knowledge experts know

Problem solving strategies particular to the subject area

Learning strategies for the subject area

Teaching methods to use:

Expert modeling

Coaching

Scaffolding (lots of structured assistance at first, gradual withdrawal of support)

Articulation by students

Reflection

Exploration

How to sequence material:

Increasing complexity

Increasing diversity

Global (the big picture) before the local (the detail)

Learning environment should emphasize:

Situated learning

Community of practice

Intrinsic motivation

Cooperation

COOPERATIVE LEARNING

Necessary elements in using cooperative learning to improve role-taking (Bridgeman, 1981)

1. Required interdependence and social reciprocity
2. Consistent opportunity to be an expert
3. Integration of varied perspectives and appreciation for the result
4. Equal status cooperation
5. Highly structured to allow easy replication of these interactions

Special Activities

GUILDELINES FOR CROSS-GRADE TUTORING

(Heath & Mangiola, 1991)

1. Allow a preparation period of at least 1 month to 6 weeks for the student tutors.

2. Use as much writing as possible in the context of the tutoring from the very beginning. Use a variety of sources and use the tutoring as a basis for tutors to write to different audiences.

3. Make field notes meaningful as a basis for conversation by providing students with occasions to share their notes orally.

4. Provide students with supportive models of open-ended questioning.

5. Emphasize the ways in which tutors can extend tutees' responses and elicit elaboration from tutees in order to impress upon them the importance of talk in learning.

6. Discuss the ways the topic relates to students' experiences.

7. Provide opportunities for tutors to prepare.

8. Develop real audiences for the students' work.

RECIPROCAL TEACHING (RT)

Context	One-on-one in laboratory settings	Groups in resource rooms	Naturally occurring groups in classrooms	Work groups fully integrated into science classrooms
Activities	Summarizing, questioning, clarifying, predicting	Gist and analogy	Complex argument structure	Thought experiments
Materials	Unconnected passages	Coherent content	Research-related resources material	Student-prepared
Pattern of use	Individual strategy training	Group discussion	Planned RT for learning content and jigsaw teaching	Opportunistic use of RT

Special Activities

ETHICAL DILEMMA DISCUSSION
(Power, Higgins, & Kohlberg, 1989; Reimer, Paolitto, & Hersh, 1983)

I. GROUP PREPARATION BY THE TEACHER

A. Build a facilitative classroom atmosphere
1. Physical arrangement. Seating arrangements of circles and squares are more conducive to discussion among peers.
2. Grouping. Dividing students into pairs or small groups (with 3-5 students) helps create trust and cooperation among students.
3. Modeling acceptance. The teacher communicating acceptance and respect for students' thoughts and feelings helps facilitate the sharing of ideas openly among students.
4. Listening and communication skills. Effective communication skills are necessary for both teachers and students. Listening skills for the teacher include checking for comprehension, asking for clarification, and encouraging elaboration.
5. Encouraging student-to-student interaction. The four previously described skills should be combined into a teacher's interaction style that encourages dialogue among the students.

B. Establish guidelines
The teacher needs to establish guidelines and rules for students to follow during moral dilemma discussions, such as requesting to speak by raising hand, respectful disagreement of other students' ideas and opinions, etc.

C. Teach discussion skills
The teacher should spend time teaching students good discussion skills if they do not yet know or practice them.

II. CONFRONTING THE DILEMMA

A. The dilemma can be presented to the students in one or more of the following ways
1. Read to the group.
2. Read individually.
3. Presented as an oral report.
4. Viewed as a media presentation (video, movie, tv show).
5. Presented as a dramatic recreation.

B. The teacher should practice the following facilitation techniques when presenting and discussing the dilemma:
1. State the central problem and action choices.
2. Give a synopsis of details.
3. Check students' comprehension periodically.
4. Clarify details when needed.
5. Define terminology when needed.

Special Activities

ETHICAL DILEMMA DISCUSSION (continued)

III. FORMULATION OF INITIAL POSITION TOWARDS THE DILEMMA

A. Students first reflect privately on the dilemma and possible action choices.

B. The students, individually, select an action choice and write it down.

C. They then select 1-2 justifications for the action they chose and write them down.

D. With teacher as facilitator, the students indicate their choices to the group (either by raising hands or given orally).

E. Students also indicate their justifications to the group, facilitated by the teacher.

F. The teacher should repeat steps B and C with another dilemma or variation if there is too much agreement on an action choice.

IV. SMALL GROUP DISCUSSIONS

A. The students are divided into small groups (n=5) according to one of these criteria:
1. Students within groups all have heterogeneous choices of action (i.e., students in the group disagree on which action should be taken to resolve the dilemma).
2. Students within groups all have homogeneous choices.
3. Students who are "undecided" form separate groups.

B. Instruct small groups by giving them specific behavioral goals:
1. Decide on the best choice and reason.
2. Decide on the best reasons for each choice.
3. Rank order the reasons from most to least favored.

C. Help facilitate small group discussion by circulating from group to group and assisting students in remaining on-task.

V. DEBATE

A. Organize a debate in front of a full group.
1. Use small group leaders for debate participants.
2. Use volunteers.

B. Get whole group to discuss and debate.
1. Students give support for one action choice.
2. Other students give rebuttal for same choice.

Special Activities

ETHICAL DILEMMA DISCUSSION (continued)

VI. FULL GROUP DISCUSSION

A. Small group reports
1. Each group gives a brief report.
2. Teacher records summary of report on the chalkboard.

B. Facilitate discussion
1. Analyze reasoning for action choices in the context of
    a. issues
    b. previous dilemmas
    c. analagous dilemmas
    d. consequences
2. Use probes to:
    a. check students' perception
    b. request definitions from students
    c. practice role-taking with student
    d. clarify particular issues
    e. consider consequences of action choice
    f. elicit reasoning behind choice
3. Dilemma variation:
    a. complicate probes with "what if" questions
    b. present a parallel dilemma
    c. add personal anecdotes
    d. relate dilemma to course content

C. Close discussion by summarizing issues raised

VII. RECONSIDERATION OF INITIAL POSITION PRIVATELY

A. The students reflect privately on the dilemma and discussion.

B. They then choose an action and write it down.

C. They give a justification for the action and write it down.

D. Students voluntarily give testimonials as to how the discusion affected their most recent action choice and reasoning.

VIII. FOLLOW-UP ASSIGNMENTS
A. The students discuss the dilemma with their family.
B. They complete a relevant reading or media viewing and relate the dilemma to it.
C. They have an interviewing project, talking to different peers/family/ community members about the dilemma and their action choice and reason.
D. They find an example of a similar dilemma with a known outcome and reason.
E. They write a solution to the dilemma in essay format.

Special Activities

THE JIGSAW METHOD
(For more information, see Aronson & Patnoe, 1997, *The Jigsaw Classroom*)

The Jigsaw Method of cooperative learning helps children work together on an equal basis. It has been shown to improve empathy for fellow students, mastery of course material, liking of school and liking of classmates.

Goal: That students treat each other as resources
Instructional outcome: Students learn that it is possible to work together without sacrificing excellence.
Structure:

> Individual competition is incompatible with success.
> Success is dependent on cooperative behavior.
> All students has unique information to bring to the group.

You must provide material written by relative experts. This could be an article broken into pieces or could be cards on which you write critical information.

1. Divide the written material into 3-6 coherent parts (could be by paragraphs).
2. Assign students to 3-5 groups.
3. Assign one part of the material to each group member.
4. Those with the same part meet in groups to learn their knowledge (10-15 minutes).
5. Group members return to their original groups to learn from their group.
6. Everyone takes a quiz on all the material.

STRUCTURED CONTROVERSY
The steps for a structured academic controversy (Johnson & Johnson, 1997) are as follows:

(1) Select an issue relevant to what you are studying. Select two or more opinions on the issue.

(2) Form advocacy teams by putting the students into groups for each different opinion. Either put together a list of supporting statements for each opinion, or have students research the opinion and come up with their own supporting statements (if this is done, provide guidance and feedback for the accuracy and comprehensiveness of the supporting statements they generate). Each group prepares a persuasive statement based on the supporting statements of their opinion.

(3) Have each group present its persuasive case to the other groups without interruption. Students in the listening groups should listen carefully and take notes to learn the other opinion well.

(4) Have open discussion among the groups with advocacy of their own position and refutation of other positions (respectfully).

(5) Groups trade positions on the issue to take another group's perspective. The group must present the other perspective to the others as sincerely and persuasively as the original group did. The group can add new facts, information, or arguments to the position (based on what they have already learned) to make it more persuasive.

(6) All individuals drop their advocacy and group-orientation to discuss the positions again and try to come to a consensus about which position is the best. The position can be one that is a synthesis of two or more, as long as the position isn't a simple compromise.

Special Activities

STRUCTURED CONTROVERSY
LESSON PLANNING SHEET

Grade Level_____   Subject area_____

Size of group_____   How groups formed_____

Room arrangement_____

Issue_____

     One perspective_____

     Second perspective_____

     Third perspective_____

Student materials required_____

Define the controversy_____

_____

_____

Ethical Judgment Appendix

Making a strategic plan for change

1. What I/we want to change:

2. The end result I/we want:

3. What is current reality—now? Identify the difference between where things stand now and where you want to get to.

4. What steps do I/we need to take to get to the desired end result? Brainstorm on methods or strategies to reach your objectives. Don't eliminate any methods or strategies at this point.

5. How will I/we know my/our actions are working? Brainstorm on ways to check that actions are or are not working.

6. Now select the best goals and the best set of steps to reach them. Make sure:
- That the goals are going to reach the end result we desire (Imagine the strategies successfully completed.)
- To quantify the goal where you can.
- To translate comparative terms (e.g., more, better, less, increased) into their actual goals.
- To create long-term, lasting results rather than just solving individual problems.
- That your goals describe an actual result rather than only a process for achieving that result.
- That your goals are specific.

Linking EJ Skills to Search Institute Assets

VIRTUE \ SUBSKILL	EJ-1 Reasoning Generally	EJ-2 Reasoning Ethically	EJ-3 Understand Problems	EJ-4 Using Codes	EJ-5 Conse-quences	EJ-6 Reflecting	EJ-7 Coping
1. Family support							
2. Positive family comm.				*			
3. Other adult relationships				*			
4. Caring neighborhood					*		
5. Caring school climate					*		
6. Parent involvement in school				*			
7. Community values youth							
8. Youth as resources					*		
9. Service to others		*				*	
10. Safety					*		
11. Family boundaries				*			
12. School boundaries				*			
13. Neighborhood boundaries				*			
14. Adult role models		*		*		*	
15. Positive peer influence		*					
16. High expectations					*		
17. Creative activities							
18. Youth programs							
19. Religious community							
20. Time at home							
21. Achievement motivation					*		*
22. School engagement							
23. Homework							
24. Bonding to school		*		*			
25. Reading for pleasure							
26. Caring		*		*	*	*	
27. Equality and social justice		*	*	*	*	*	
28. Integrity		*				*	
29. Honesty		*		*		*	
30. Responsibility		*		*	*	*	
31. Restraint		*			*	*	*
32. Planning and decision making	*	*	*	*	*	*	*
33. Interpersonal competence				*	*		
34. Cultural competence		*		*		*	
35. Resistance skills		*			*	*	*
36. Peaceful conflict resolution							*
37. Personal power							*
38. Self-esteem							*
39. Sense of purpose				*	*		*
40. Positive view of personal future							*

Recommended Resources for Character Education

De Vries, R., & Zan, B. S. (1994). *Moral classrooms, moral children: Creating a constructivist atmosphere in early education.* New York: Teachers College Press.

Elias, M. J., Arnold, H., & Hussey, C. S. (Eds.). (2002). *EQ + IQ = Best leadership practices for caring and successful schools.* Thousand Oaks, CA: Corwin Press

Gootman, M. E. (2008). *The caring teacher's guide to discipline: Helping students learn self-control, responsibility, and respect, K-6* (3rd ed.). Thousand Oaks, CA: Corwin Press.

Greene, A. (1996). *Rights to responsibility: Multiple approaches to developing character and community.* Tucson, AZ: Zephyr.

Jweid, R., & Rizzo, M. (2001). *Building character through literature: A guide for middle school readers.* Lanham, MD: Scarecrow.

Kirschenbaum, H. (1994). *100 ways to enhance values and morality in schools and youth meetings.* Boston: Allyn & Bacon.

Lantieri, L., & Goleman, D. (2008). *Building emotional intelligence: Techniques to cultivate inner strength in children.* Boulder, CO: Sounds True, Incorporated.

Liebling, C. R. (1986). *Inside view and character plans in original stories and their basal reader adaptations.* Washington, DC: National Institute of Education.

Miller, J. C., & Clarke, C. (1998). *10-minute life lessons for kids: 52 fun and simple games and activities to teach your child trust, honesty, love, and other important values.* New York: HarperPerennial Library.

Nucci, L. P., & Narvaez, D. (Eds.). (2008). *Handbook of moral and character education.* New York: Routledge.

Power, F. C., Nuzzi, R. J., Narvaez, D., Lapsley, D. K., & Hunt, T. C. (Eds.). (2008). *Moral education: A handbook* (Vols. 1-2). Westport, CT: Praeger.

Ryan, K. A., & Bohlin, K. E. (2000). *Building character in schools: Practical ways to bring moral instruction to life.* San Francisco: Jossey-Bass.

Ryan, K., & Wynne, E. A. (1996). *Reclaiming our schools: Teaching character, academics, and discipline.* Upper Saddle River, NJ: Prentice Hall.

Watson, M., & Eckert, L. (2003). *Learning to trust.* San Francisco: Jossey-Bass.

Resources/References for Ethical Judgment

ETHICAL DILEMMA RESOURCES
with sample dilemma

For current ethical issues and dilemmas, consult the following websites:

The Institute of Global Ethics, http://www.globalethics.org
Website includes descriptions of moral dilemmas in several different areas
(e.g., business, medical, education, etc.). See sample moral dilemma below
from website.

Ethics Updates, http://ethics.sandiego.edu
Website includes current ethical issues (e.g., world hunger, death penalty,
animal rights, etc.) and links to articles explaining these issues and/or taking
a position on them.

Sample moral dilemma
(from The Institute of Global Ethics, http://www.globalethics.org)

"The Dying Passenger"

Short Version
A pilot, caught in a winter storm over the Midwest, must choose between
making an emergency landing to save the life of a passenger, or protecting his
crew and passengers by continuing the flight.

Extended Version
Mike Nolan knew there was a problem even before the flight attendant
knocked on the cockpit door. After 18 years of piloting 747s and their smaller
kin across the country and around the world, Nolan had developed a keen
sense of the atmosphere aboard his planes. This flight—a December trip from
Detroit to Seattle—had been a struggle from the start.

First, there had been the late departure from the Detroit gate—a delay caused
by a flat tire on the food-service van a few miles from the gate. The van's
driver had been further slowed by the onset of a snowstorm, whose first flur-
ries had begun falling less than an hour before. Compounding the slow start
was the packed and cramped cabin to Nolan's back, a precursor to the coming
holiday crunch. The flight crew was new, too—each with plenty of experience,
but not yet used to one another as a routine team on this westbound route.
These things—more disruptive and disjointed than truly troubling—had nevertheless put Nolan on alert.

So when the knock came on the cockpit door, Nolan wasn't entirely unpre-
pared. At the door was Maggie Cho, a flight attendant Mike had worked with a
few times before, although not on this route. Maggie, Nolan knew, was new to
the route and relatively new to the job, but had the bearings and the brains to
stay calm in a crisis—qualifications that made her a good person to have in
the cabin. Tonight, Mike soon realized, she was badly needed.

Resources/References for Ethical Judgment

Extended version of Sample Dilemma (continued)

Maggie wasted no time in telling Nolan and the rest of the cockpit crew that there was trouble in the back: A passenger had suffered a severe heart attack and needed immediate medical attention. While a doctor aboard the plane had been able to help, a hospital was needed quickly—or the patient would likely die.

Nolan knew his options were few and his time short. The scheduled flight path had led Nolan's plane slightly south in a bid to slip the grip of a growing snowstorm over the northern plains. That tactic, however, had failed. The storm, pushed and pulled by competing air-pressure systems, had spread more widely than forecast, covering America's middle states with a wide swath of snow, sleet, and strong winds. And Nolan's night flight, now 20 minutes from Denver, was in the middle of the mess.

Transferring control to his copilot, Mike took to the radio, calling the Denver tower to seek clearance for an emergency landing. From the other end of the radio, Nolan heard a pained response: Permission denied. The Denver controller explained that weather conditions were worsening, making a landing unadvisable and unsafe for Nolan's crew and passengers. With extreme regret, the Denver tower told Nolan to provide what medical care he could—but to continue his flight as prescribed.

Mike, Maggie, and the rest of the cockpit crew looked at each other, pained expressions on their faces. After talking quietly for a few minutes, Mike concretized their options: They could follow Denver's orders and stay aloft, or they could demand a landing for a medical evacuation.

The weather WAS a problem, Mike admitted, but not one he wasn't ready to meet. Nolan felt sure he could land the plane—a confidence borne of 27 years' experience at the controls of military and civilian aircraft. But he wasn't prepared to risk the lives of his crew and passengers—breaking the conservative standards of airline safety regulations—without their full and informed consent.

At Mike's request, Maggie returned to the cabin for a status check. In less than three minutes, she was back with bad news: The patient's condition was worsening. News of the crisis, she said, had spread remarkably slowly, running through only a small portion of the passenger cabin. The rest of the flight crew, however, had been told of the emergency and had—with only one fleeting hold out—signaled their wish to land the plane immediately.

Now, the choice was Nolan's.

Resources/References for Ethical Judgment

CITIZENSHIP RESOURCES

Character Education Partnership
918 16th Street NW, Suite 501
Washington, DC 20006
800 988-8081
www.character.org
Description: Character Education Partnership's (CEP) Online Database has character education resources and organizations, scroll through material from CEP's Character Education Resource Guide, or view a list of other character education web sites.

National Council for Social Studies
3501 Newark Street NW
Washington, DC 20016
800 683-0812
http://www.socialstudies.org
Description: The mission of National Council for the Social Studies (NCSS) is to provide leadership, service, and support for all social studies educators, who teach students the content knowledge, intellectual skills, and civic values necessary for fulfilling the duties of citizenship in a participatory democracy. NCSS offers teaching resources in many areas of social studies, including civic ideals and practices and power, authority, and governance.

U.S. House of Representatives web site
www.house.gov
Description: Students can learn about the U.S. House of Representatives.

Resources/References for Ethical Judgment

Angers, T. (1999). *The forgotten hero of My Lai: The Hugh Thompson story*. Lafayette, LA: Acadian House.

Aronson, E., & Patnoe, S. (1997). *The jigsaw classroom: Building cooperation in the classroom*. New York: Longman.

Armstrong, W. (1989). *Sounder*. New York: Harper & Row.

Asturias, M. (1968). *Strong wind*. New York: Delacorte Press.

Begun, R.W. (1996). *Ready-to-use social skills lessons & activities for grades 4-6*. West Nyack, NY: Center for Applied Research in Education.

Braine, M. D. S. (1990). The "natural logic" approach to reasoning. In W. F. Overton (Ed.), *Reasoning, necessity, and logic: Developmental perspectives* (pp. 135-158). Hillsdale, NJ: Erlbaum.

Bransford, J., Sherwood, R., Rieser, J., & Vye, N. (1986). Teaching thinking and problem solving: Research foundations. *American Psychologist, 41*, 1078-1089.

Bransford, J., & Stein, B. (1984). *The IDEAL problem solver*. New York: Freeman

Bridgeman, D. (1981). Enhanced role-taking through cooperative interdependence: A field study. *Child Development, 52*, 1231-1238.

Calne, D. B. (1999). *Within reason*. New York: Pantheon.

Campolo, A., & Aeschliman, G. (1992). *50 ways you can help save the planet*. Downer's Grove, IL: InterVarsity Press.

Collins, A., Hawkins, J., & Carver. S. (1991). *A cognitive apprenticeship for disadvantaged students*. Washington, DC: U.S. Department of Education.

Collins, W.(1999). *The moonstone*. New York: Oxford University Press.

Ellis, S., & Siegler, R. S. (1994). Development of problem solving. In R. J. Sternberg (Ed.), *Thinking and problem solving* (pp. 334-368). New York: Academic Press.

Ennis, R. H. (1987). A taxonomy of critical thinking dispositions and abilities. In J. Baron & R. Sternberg (Eds.), *Teaching thinking skills: Theory and practice*. New York: Freeman.

Forni, P. (2002). *Choosing civility: The twenty-five rules of considerate conduct*. New York: St. Martin's Press.

Fox, P. (1984). *One-eyed cat*. Scarsdale, NY: Bradbury.

Gibbs, J., Potter, G., & Goldstein, A. (1995). *The EQUIP program: Teaching youth to think and act responsibly through a peer-helping approach*. Champaign, IL: Research Press.

Golding, W. (1962). *Lord of the flies*. New York: Coward-McCann.

Gutmann, A., & Thompson, D. (1996). *Democracy and disagreement*. Cambridge, MA: Belknap Press.

Haan, N., Aerts, E., & Cooper, B. (1985). *On moral grounds: The search for practical morality*. New York: New York University Press.

Hart, D. (1988). A longitudinal study of adolescents' socialization and identification as predictors of adult moral judgment development. *Merrill-Palmer Quarterly, 34*(3), 245-260.

Heath, S., & Mangiola, L. (1991). *Children of promise: Literate activity in linguistically and culturally diverse classrooms*. Washington, DC: National Education Association.

Holroyd, K., & Lazarus, R. (1982). Stress, coping, and somatic adaptation. In L. Goldberger & S. Breznitz (Eds.), *Handbook of stress: Theoretical and clinical aspects*. New York: Free Press.

Hugo, V. (1982). *Les miserables*. New York: Penguin.

Johnson, D. W. (1993). *Reaching out*. New York: Allyn & Bacon.

Johnson, D. W., & Johnson, F. P. (1997). *Joining together*. Boston: Allyn & Bacon.

Kidder, R. M. (1995). *How good people make tough choices: Resolving the dilemmas of ethical living*. New York: Morrow.

(continued)

Mann, L., Harmoni, R., & Power, C. (1991). The GOFER course in decision-making. In J. Baron & R. Brown (Eds.), *Teaching decision-making to adolescents* (pp. 61-78). Hillsdale, NJ: Lawrence Erlbaum.

Myers, W. (1988). *Scorpions.* New York: Harper Collins.

Myers, W. (1992). *Somewhere in the darkness.* New York: Scholastic.

Marzano, R. J., Brandt, R. S., Hughes, C. S., Jones, B. F., Presseisen, B. Z., Rankin, S. C., Suhor, C. (1988). *Dimensions of thinking: A framework for curriculum and instruction.* Alexandria, VA: Association for Supervision and Curriculum Development.

McCullough, M., & Sealy, K. (1986). *Brown eyes, blue eyes.* Birmingham, AL: New Hope.

McGraw, J. (2000). *Life strategies for teens.* New York: Fireside.

Naylor, P. (1991). *Shiloh.* New York: Atheneum.

Oliner, S. P., & Oliner, P. M. (1988). *The altruistic personality: Rescuers of Jews in Nazi Europe.* New York: The Free Press.

Overton, W. F. (Ed.). (1990). *Reasoning, necessity, and logic: Developmental perspectives.* Hillsdale, NJ: Erlbaum.

Peale, N. V. (1952). *The power of positive thinking.* New York: Prentice-Hall.

Power, C., Higgins, A., & Kohlberg, L. (1989). *Lawrence Kohlberg's approach to moral education.* New York: Columbia University Press.

Pratkanis, A., & Aronson, E. (1992). *Age of propaganda: The everyday use and abuse of persuasion.* New York: W. H. Freeman.

Pratt, M. W., Norris, J. E., Arnold, M. L., & Filyer, R. (1999). Generativity and moral development as predictors of value-socialization narratives for young persons across the adult life span: From lessons learned to stories shared. *Psychology & Aging, 14*(3), 414-426.

Reimer, J., Paolitto, D., & Hersh, R. (1983). *Promoting moral growth: From Piaget to Kohlberg.* New York: Longman.

Rest, J. R., & Narvaez, D. (Eds.). (1994). *Moral development in the professions: Psychology and applied ethics.* Hillsdale, NJ: Erlbaum.

Ross, W. D. R. (1939). *Foundations of ethics.* Oxford: Clarendon Press.

Sagan, C. (1997). *The demon-haunted world: Science as a candle in the dark.* New York: Ballantine Books.

Schonert-Reichl, K. A. (1999). Relations of peer acceptance, friendship adjustment, and social behavior to moral reasoning during early adolescence. *Journal of Early Adolescence, 19*(2), 249-279.

Seligman, M. E. P. (1995). *The optimistic child.* New York: HarperCollins.

Silverstein, S. (2004). *The giving tree.* New York: HarperCollins Juvenile.

Sternberg, R. J. (1981). Nothing fails like success: The search for an intelligent paradigm for studying intelligence. *Journal of Educational Psychology, 73,* 142-155.

Thoma, S. (1994). Moral judgment and moral action. In J. R. Rest & D. Narvaez (Eds.), *Moral development in the professions: Psychology and applied ethics* (pp. 199-212). Hillsdale, NJ: Erlbaum.

Wade, C., & Tavris, C. (1993). *Critical and creative thinking.* New York: HarperCollins.

Walvoord, B., & Anderson, V. (1998). *Effective grading: A tool for learning and assessment.* San Francisco: Jossey-Bass.

Waters, V. (1982). Therapies for children: Rational-emotive therapy. In G. R. Reynolds & T. B. Gutkin (Eds.), *Handbook of school psychology* (pp. 570–579). New York: John Wiley.

Wheeler, D., & Janis, I. (1980). *A practical guide for making decisions.* New York: Free Press.

Ethical Judgment Appendix

About the Authors

Darcia Narvaez, Ph.D., Associate Professor of Psychology at the University of Notre Dame, developed the Integrative Ethical Education model (initiated under the federally-funded Minnesota Community Voices and Character Education Project which she reported on at a Whitehouse conference). Previously at the University of Minnesota, she was executive director of the Center for the Study of Ethical Development and was director of the Center for Ethical Education at the University of Notre Dame. She is on the editorial boards of the Journal of Educational Psychology and the Journal of Moral Education. She has published in the Journal of Educational Psychology, Developmental Psychology, and has two award-winning books, *Postconventional Moral Thinking* (1999; with Rest, Bebeau & Thoma) and *Moral Development, Self and Identity* (2004; with Lapsley).

Tonia Bock, Ph.D., Assistant Professor of Psychology at the University of St. Thomas, is an educational and developmental psychologist. She has a Master of Arts in educational policy and administration from the University of Minnesota and a Ph.D. in developmental psychology from the University of Notre Dame. She specializes in how adolescents (late elementary through college-age students) understand moral problems and situations and see themselves as moral beings. She is interested in the developmental trends of their understanding as well as what factors are related to their moral cognition.

9 780981 950112